Dyslexia and Your Newly Diagnosed Child

Dyslexia and Your Newly Diagnosed Child

Parenting Essentials, Tips, and Strategies to Help Your Child

Rebecca Bush, CALT, LDT

Zeitgeist • New York

To Mom, for your unshakable belief in me, your boundless love, and your endless determination to fight for every opportunity possible for us

This book is designed to provide helpful information on the subjects discussed. It is not meant to be used for, nor should it take the place of, diagnosing or treating any medical conditions. Please consult a physician or mental health professional before adopting any exercises or guidelines. The publisher and author are not responsible for any health needs that may require supervision or consultation with a licensed and qualified health-care provider.

Zeitgeist™
An imprint and division of Penguin Random House LLC
1745 Broadway, New York, NY 10019
zeitgeistpublishing.com
penguinrandomhouse.com

ISBN: 9798217151431
Ebook ISBN: 9798217151424

Printed in the United States of America

1st Printing

Illustrations © by Shutterstock.com
Book design by William Mack
Author photograph © by Emily Jaschke
Edited by Caroline Lee

The authorized representative in the EU for product safety and compliance is Penguin Random House Ireland, Morrison Chambers, 32 Nassau Street, Dublin D02 YH68, Ireland. https://eu-contact.penguin.ie

Contents

Introduction

Welcome, parents and caregivers! A transformational new chapter in your child's learning journey has just begun. Their diagnosis of dyslexia has undoubtedly unlocked a range of emotions. You may be feeling relief, as you now understand why your six- to nine-year-old has been struggling to learn to read, or grappling with more difficult emotions like worry, overwhelm, and confusion. You may be concerned that your child may not develop a love of reading and are unsure where to go from here. Rest assured, whatever you're feeling is normal. A child with dyslexia just needs the right help—and so do you. This next phase does not have to be faced alone.

I'm on a mission to change the landscape of literacy and dyslexia education, and I'm a passionate advocate for empowering learners with dyslexia and their families. For almost two decades, I've worked in the education field with people of all ages and at all stages who face dyslexia and other challenges, such as cognitive functioning difficulties and language-processing disorders. In my private practice as a dyslexia interventionist, academic language therapist, and reading specialist, I create tailored, intensive intervention programs for struggling readers, and I coach families just like yours. With the right approach and consistency, every single one of my students has learned to read and every single parent or caregiver has felt empowered to support their child.

The road ahead will be bumpy. You and your child will sometimes feel frustrated, but fortunately, we live in a modern world where research and technology have shown us exactly what's needed to support your child's development as a reader. The journey may be long, but with the help of the strategies in this book, you can create a road map to success for your child. We know the right path forward, and you are setting your child on it. They will learn to read, unlock their personal strengths, feel the thrill of independence, love stories, and know how to advocate for themselves. They will. I promise.

Dyslexia and Your Newly Diagnosed Child is thoughtfully designed to help you gain a deeper understanding of what dyslexia is and, more important, help you recognize your child's strengths and the challenges they will face. With this knowledge, you'll be equipped to dive into practical strategies you can confidently apply in your daily lives. These strategies cover literacy and language skills, social and emotional development, cognitive and other academic skills, plus sensory and motor integration, empowering you to help your child's reading skills develop, nurture their love of learning, and reinforce their confidence as they grow.

This is the beginning of a promising new phase in your child's life. You already have explanations and now it's time to find solutions.

How to Use This Book

This book is divided into two parts:

Part I summarizes dyslexia, child development, and the challenges your child may be facing and provides a solid foundation to start from. This information will help you implement the strategies in part II, so it's best to read this part first.

Part II addresses specific developmental areas and offers bite-sized strategies to support a variety of challenges seen in learners with dyslexia. Feel free to hop right to the chapter you believe will most benefit your child, but do review them all—see what works, see what doesn't. Your child might be struggling in an area you didn't suspect.

Dyslexia is a reading challenge, but it can impact other areas and coexist with other diagnoses. So, in addition to strategies to improve literacy and language skills, you'll find a range of techniques to support your whole child. Each strategy in part II is evidence- and/or research-based.

The chapters in part II cover everything you need to know to implement the strategies:

Background information helps you contextualize your child's experience.

Step-by-step instructions empower you to put the strategies into action.

Troubleshooting tips provide additional support.

Sidebars throughout help you more fully understand your child's journey.

Remember, this book is your guide, so make it your own. Give yourself the grace and space to try something new. Learn, apply, and readjust as needed. Each chapter concludes with an invitation to reflect on your progress and celebrate the successes. You can do this—so let's get started!

PART I

Before You Begin

1

Fundamentals

Dyslexia can present in different ways for different people, and you may hear slightly different terms. This learning process may seem complex and overwhelming to navigate, but the better you understand dyslexia, the better able you'll be to successfully support your child. In this chapter, you'll learn what dyslexia is (and what it isn't), what impact it has, what coexisting conditions may occur, and what effective interventions exist.

What Is Dyslexia?

To put your mind at ease from the get-go, let's debunk some misinformation about dyslexia and replace it with these research-based truths:

- Dyslexia has nothing to do with how smart your child is or how hard they work.
- Dyslexia is *not* related to poor vision or "seeing letters backward."
- Your child will *not* outgrow dyslexia, so a wait-and-see approach is detrimental.
- Dyslexia occurs in both boys and girls at similar rates.

- Dyslexia occurs in other languages, not just English.
- Colored overlays or special glasses are *not* effective for dyslexia.
- Vision therapy and brain-training programs *won't* help someone with dyslexia.
- Dyslexia is *not* caused by bad teaching, but it can worsen or perpetuate the symptoms. (The term for this scenario is "dysteachia.")
- With the right instruction, a child with dyslexia *will* learn to read.

Thanks to decades of research, we know exactly what dyslexia is. While our understanding is always expanding and definitions may differ and change, here's the definition I'll use, based on the International Dyslexia Association's definition and other current research at the time this book was published:

> *Dyslexia is a specific learning disability that primarily impacts one's ability to accurately read words or decode.*
>
> *A lifelong disorder, it is neurobiological in origin and often characterized by difficulties with phonological processing, which can lead to additional challenges in reading fluency, reading comprehension, and/or encoding.*
>
> *These challenges exist despite sufficient cognitive abilities and adequate educational opportunities. It is not related to vision problems or lack of motivation.*
>
> *Dyslexia exists on a continuum and is sometimes referred to by different terms.*

Let's break that down and elaborate:

Dyslexia is a specific learning disability that impacts:

- Accurate and/or fluent word recognition
- Reading at the word level
- Decoding (breaking apart, sounding out, and reading words)
- Often, encoding (spelling words)

Dyslexia is a lifelong disorder. Your child will not outgrow dyslexia, but the symptoms may look different depending on what intervention they've received and where they are in their learning journey.

Dyslexia is neurobiological. This refers to the biological processes and structures of the brain and nervous system. This also means dyslexia is hereditary and runs in families. In fact, a child of a parent with dyslexia has almost a 50/50 chance of having dyslexia.

Dyslexia is characterized by difficulties with phonological processing. This refers to an individual's ability to recognize and manipulate the speech sounds that make up words.

Dyslexia exists despite having nothing to do with intelligence, motivation, or vision problems. Therefore, dyslexia is unexpected.

Dyslexia exists on a continuum ranging from mild to severe. Dyslexia can look different for everyone, and therefore, no two people will have exactly the same symptoms.

Dyslexia may be referred to by different terms. While the term "dyslexia" is widely used, you may hear other terms such as:

- Developmental dyslexia: Researchers sometimes use this term to differentiate from "acquired dyslexia."
- Acquired dyslexia: This term refers to a type of dyslexia that can result from a traumatic brain injury.
- Learning difference: This term refers to a variation in how someone processes and understands information, impacting how they learn to read, write, or do math.
- Specific learning disability in reading: This is the legal definition, which is often used in schools.
- Specific learning disorder with impairment in reading: Psychologists often use this official term from the *Diagnostic and Statistical Manual of Mental Disorders, Fifth Edition* (DSM-V).

If that isn't enough to cause some confusion, you may notice that "disability" and "disorder" are sometimes used interchangeably. While similar, they do carry slightly different meanings. "Disability" is the legal term, while "disorder" is the medical or neurodevelopmental term. No matter the terms, you'll approach your child's dyslexia by choosing the most helpful strategies for their particular challenges.

Visualizing Dyslexia

Dyslexia exists on a continuum because each person experiences different levels of difficulty with reading. The visual of a continuum highlights the reality that while the definition of dyslexia doesn't change, it's not a one-size-fits-all disorder. While you'll hear psychologists describe dyslexia as mild, moderate, or severe (see diagram that follows), there is nuance and variation within those categories. Using psychoeducational and evaluation assessments, an evaluator will determine the intensity of the impairment in reading.

The Dyslexia Continuum

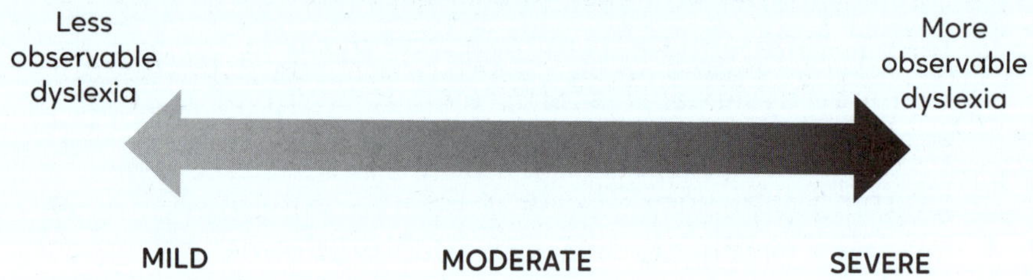

The double arrows are helpful to show the varying ranges of intensity, but I prefer to think of dyslexia as concentric circles as demonstrated in the diagram below because each person will experience each difficulty differently. We know the cause and symptoms of dyslexia, but everyone—including your child—is unique. We'll walk through the parts of the wheel as we move through this chapter.

The Dyslexia Wheel

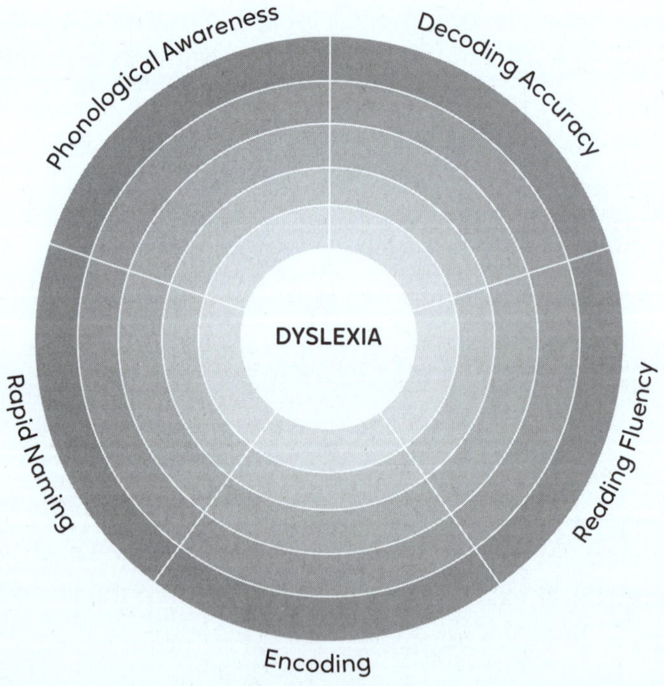

Are There Different Types of Dyslexia?

There's only one type of dyslexia, but since it impacts different parts of the brain to different degrees and presents differently in people, it can seem like there's more than one type. Plus, experts may talk about it in various ways, making the topic more challenging to understand. However, true dyslexia is characterized by difficulty with word-level reading and often spelling, which is typically caused by a phonological deficit, or difficulty processing the sounds of language.

That said, someone with dyslexia could have other deficits, too, such as language-processing challenges or poor working memory skills, which can make the symptoms of dyslexia worse. This is actually very common, and we'll look more closely at it throughout this book.

While some argue that there are no established subtypes and that dyslexia is a continuum of reading difficulties with each individual's experience being slightly different, you may see the terms "surface dyslexia" or "double-deficit dyslexia" to describe dyslexia's impact. These are labels that can be used to describe parts of the dyslexia continuum.

Surface dyslexia (aka orthographic dyslexia) may be used to refer to someone who can decode regularly spelled words but struggles with irregularly spelled words. For example, "ship" can be read accurately, but "taught" may not be.

Double-deficit dyslexia may refer to someone who has a phonological deficit and a rapid naming deficit. A rapid naming deficit makes it difficult for someone to quickly pull up the name of something. Even if they know the word, the brain just takes a little longer to say it.

Some experts incorrectly add reading comprehension difficulties to the definition of dyslexia, but that's a different challenge. A reading comprehension disorder means that the child can read everything accurately, but they struggle to understand what they read. A struggle with reading comprehension can be a knock-on effect of dyslexia, but it is not dyslexia. The diagram below shows how the following three key deficits could overlap in struggling readers:

- Phonological deficit
- Rapid naming deficit
- Language comprehension deficit

Remember, your child is unique and all the terms in this section may rightly seem confusing, so just focus on how you can support your child with the best intervention strategies possible.

The Overlap of Key Deficits in Struggling Readers

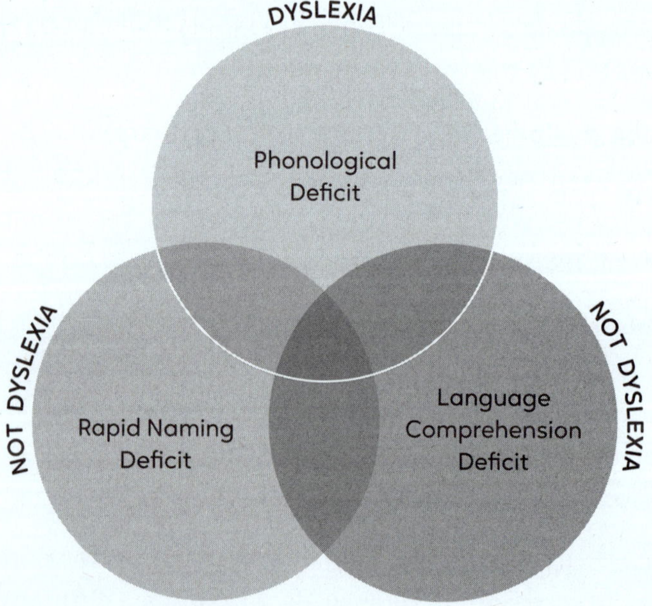

The Mechanics of Dyslexia

As mentioned before, dyslexia impacts how your child's brain processes information; it's typically a deficit in the brain's ability to process the individual sounds and chunks of sounds in our language, also known as the phonological component of language.

Dyslexia negatively affects how your child learns to correctly decode, or break down, words, which can affect their other literacy skills, such as fluency, reading comprehension, and spelling. This makes it difficult for your child to learn certain skills because the brain takes in and works with information in an unexpected way. Rest assured, however, the intervention methods you'll learn in this book can help rewire these unexpected paths and target specific areas that need to be strengthened.

Written language is a human invention, so our brains need to learn how to process it. The human brain, being both adaptive and intelligent, does this by using different parts of the brain to create a "reading pathway." This pathway allows us to:

1. Match the image (grapheme) we see to . . .
2. the sound (phoneme) we hear to . . .
3. the meaning of the word.

When we accurately make those correspondences and add them all together, we are reading. For example, to read the word "cat," we must know the sound each letter makes. We also need to know how to blend those sounds together. Plus, we need to know what a cat is. For a skilled reader, this happens almost instantaneously.

The Reading Pathway

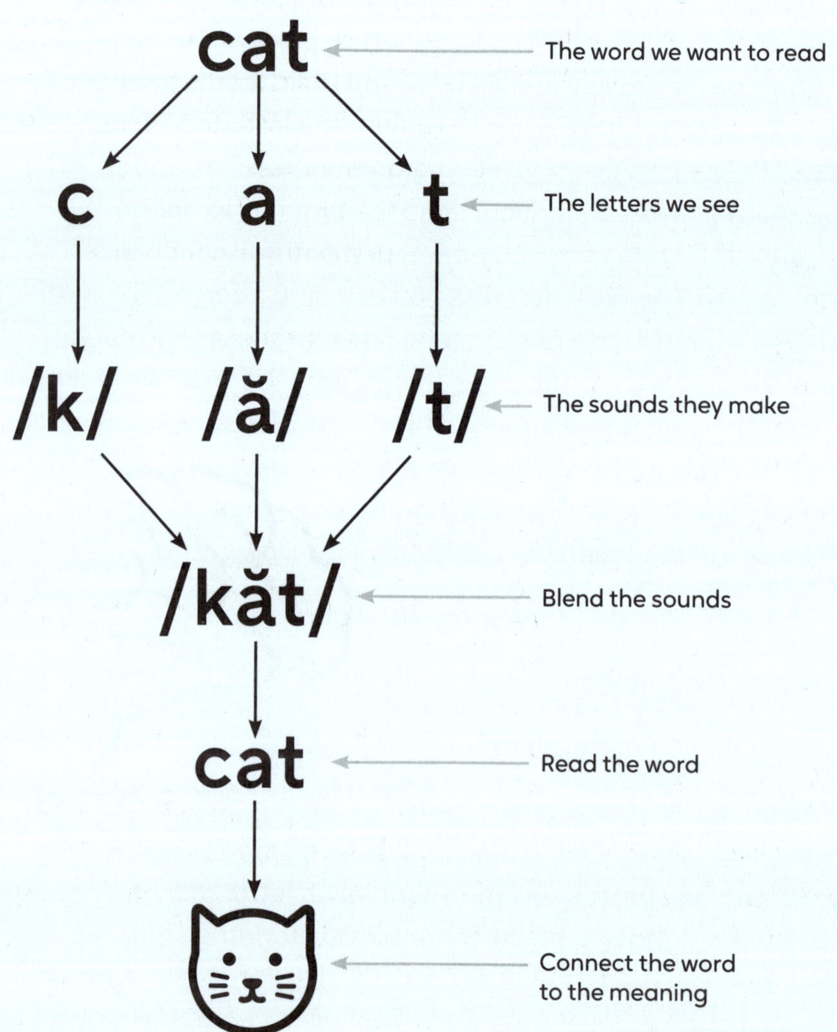

For a child with dyslexia, the reading pathway is less efficient. The map of the left hemisphere of a brain shows that, when reading, multiple parts of a typical brain are activated, whereas a dyslexic brain usually over-relies on only one area.

Thanks to neuroimaging, we know exactly what's going on in the brain of someone with dyslexia. We can see which parts of the brain activate, or don't, and which parts are under-developed. It all boils down to how the brain works when a person with dyslexia is asked to match the letters on the page to the sounds they represent. The great news is that effective intervention can essentially rewire the brain of someone with dyslexia, creating more efficient neural pathways for reading.

Comparison of Reading Activity in the Brain

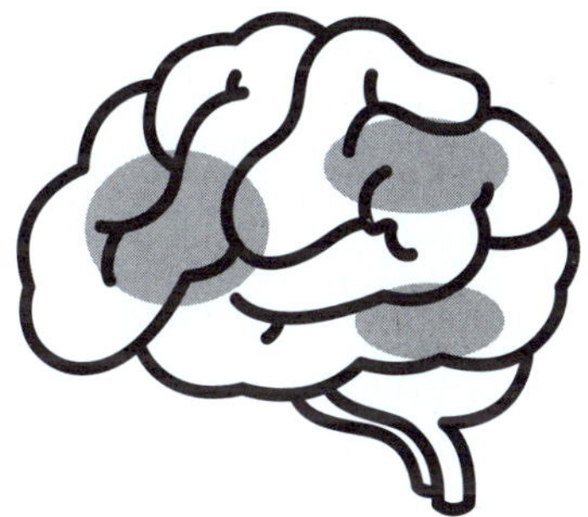

Non-impaired Reader

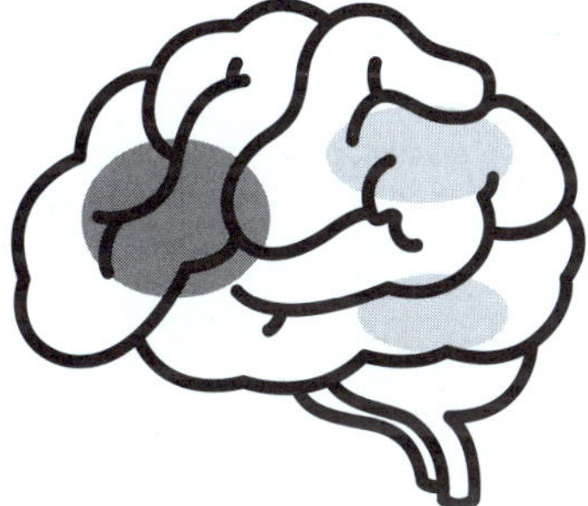

Reader with Dyslexia

Based on *Overcoming Dyslexia: Second Edition* by Drs. Sally and Jonathan Shaywitz (2020)

The Symptoms of Dyslexia

Learning to read requires instruction and practice and usually occurs at distinct stages of development. Let's start with a look at the typical process of learning to read to help you better understand the symptoms of dyslexia that challenge your child.

We'll look at the first three of the five stages of reading development from *Proust and the Squid: The Story and Science of the Reading Brain* by Maryanne Wolf on page 21. These are paired with cognitive and language development to give you the full picture.

Let's now look at how dyslexia can impact this developmental process for language, reading, and writing areas, beginning with the age of the novice reader on page 22. While dyslexia may look different from person to person and its impact can change over time, dyslexia generally presents as difficulty with:

- Decoding (breaking apart, sounding out, and reading words)
- Fluency (reading smoothly, with few mistakes and with expression, or like a conversation)
- Encoding (spelling words)

Typical Process of Learning to Read

	STAGE 1 **The emerging pre-reader**	STAGE 2 **The novice reader**	STAGE 3 **The decoding reader**
	Ages 6 months–6 years	Ages 6–7	Ages 7–9
READING DEVELOPMENT	Absorbs a love of books. Learns that text carries meaning. Pretends to read.	Learns the relationship between letters and sounds. Breaks the alphabetic code and begins to read. By late stage 2, can read up to 600 words.	Reads with increasing fluency. Masters breaking apart and reading longer words. Builds reading comprehension strategies.
COGNITIVE DEVELOPMENT	Sensory and motor regions of the brain are mostly developed. The reading pathway may not be fully developed yet.	Thinks in concrete ways. Develops a basic sense of time. Builds skills to be more independent.	Is more self-aware. Begins to understand multiple points of view.
LANGUAGE DEVELOPMENT	Learns to rhyme and play with the sounds of language. By late stage 1, all sounds can be accurately produced when speaking.	By late stage 2, can understand 4,000 words or more. Follows multistep instructions. Begins to speak with more complex sentences.	Listening comprehension remains higher than reading comprehension. Is mastering how to use language for various purposes. Begins to develop an understanding of figurative language.

The Impact of Dyslexia on Language, Reading, and Writing

	Ages 6–7	Ages 8–9
LANGUAGE	Has difficulty learning rhymes and skills related to recognizing and the ability to hear and play with the sounds in spoken words. Mispronounces words. Struggles to find the right word when talking, or rapid naming. Has trouble remembering new words.	Continues to experience the same difficulties without much progress. Has difficulty understanding idioms and puns.
READING	Has difficulty learning letter names. Has difficulty remembering the sounds letters make. Has difficulty breaking apart and putting together sounds in words. Guesses or replaces words when reading. Over-relies on pictures when reading.	Avoids reading or becomes anxious. Confuses, skips, or replaces words when reading. Has difficulty reading new words and trouble remembering words already read. Has difficulty understanding what was read.
WRITING	Confuses letters that look and sound similar. (See "Letter Reversals" on page 23.) Struggles with spelling.	Has issues with spelling, such as spelling the same word multiple ways in the same writing piece. Writing may be disorganized or difficult to understand.

Letter Reversals

A common myth is that a reader with dyslexia sees letters backward. While dyslexia has nothing to do with how your child sees letters and words on the page, "letter reversals" do happen. In fact, reversing similar letters like "b" and "d" is a completely typical part of learning to read and write. Almost all children confuse these letters at some point, and some may continue to regularly reverse letters through first grade.

This happens because of how the brain works and the visual and phonemic similarities between these letters and their corresponding sounds. The human brain has the unique ability to generalize what we know. This means we see an upside-down object as the same object. If you turn a chair upside down, you still know it's a chair. Commonly confused letters like "b" and "d" look incredibly similar—they're the same shapes after all, just flipped.

The brain is so clever that when a young child is first learning to differentiate between "b" and "d," they have to train their brain to recognize that these are, in fact, different letters. This process takes time, so it is absolutely normal for young learners to reverse letters. What's more, these two letters sound almost identical. The phonemes, or sounds of the letters (represented with the letter bookended by slashes), /b/ and /d/ are very similar.

For a child with dyslexia, who has a phonological processing deficit, it's even harder to differentiate between letters like these. When the underlying sounds are confusing and the images attached to each sound look similar, it's no wonder that letter reversals are a symptom of dyslexia.

Evaluation Areas

Here is a breakdown of what the evaluation process for dyslexia includes so you can refer to your child's assessment as needed. This information will also be helpful for a reassessment, which happens every three years for learners in the public school system. The evaluation areas observed and/or tested include:

- Intelligence (full-scale IQ): a combination of cognitive abilities (language processing, visual-spatial abilities, working memory, and processing speed)
- Phonological processing (phonological awareness, memory, and rapid naming)
- Academic achievement (reading, mathematics, writing, and oral language)
- Background information (behavior, educational history, family history, clinical, or other observations)

Other areas may be assessed to rule out other conditions or disorders, for example:

- Language abilities (expressive and receptive)
- Visual-motor functioning
- Executive functioning skills and attention
- Handwriting
- Hearing and vision
- Anxiety
- Social skills

The Occasional Mismatch between Academic Demands and Child Development

There's more academic pressure on students than ever before, starting even before kindergarten, as university requirements and the job market have become increasingly more competitive over the past several decades. Kids your child's age shouldn't have to feel this pressure, but they likely do. Because of this increase in expectations, sometimes child development just doesn't match what a school asks students to accomplish. Sure, some students will meet or even exceed these expectations, but many may not. Plus, a child's cognitive, linguistic, or motor development may not yet be advanced enough for them to successfully meet a school's requirements.

For your child with dyslexia, it's essential to step back from what the school may be expecting and examine what is developmentally appropriate, and possible, at your child's age and stage. While you can think realistically about what's possible for your child at any point, you never want to wait to see what will happen as your child grows. Early intervention is essential and there are distinct developmentally appropriate windows to consider as well.

To get a better idea of how to assess academic requirements for your child's school, you can review developmental milestones, such as the Centers for Disease Control and Prevention's Developmental Milestones (up to age five), or your state's education standards. You can also compare your child's school to other schools. Additionally, make sure to observe your child's stress levels. Oftentimes, if a learner is anxious or not interested, the material may just be too hard. You can also consult with a professional who specializes in child development to help provide a big-picture perspective.

Other Challenges That May Coexist with Dyslexia

"Comorbidity" sounds serious, but it just means that two or more conditions or disorders coexist in the same person. It's key for you and your child to understand that they may face other challenges on top of, or as secondary consequences of, their dyslexia. Getting the right kind of support can make all the difference.

You may have learned of coexisting conditions in your child during their evaluation, but it's also possible the evaluator was focused solely on dyslexia or that your child may display other challenges along their journey. It's commonly accepted that 30 to 60 percent of people with dyslexia have one or more coexisting conditions. So, if your child is struggling in other areas, they're not alone. Let's look at some of these common challenges.

Other Specific Learning Disorders

Dyslexia is one of three specific learning disorders. The other two are:

Dysgraphia: difficulty with writing

Dyscalculia: difficulty with math

Like dyslexia, these disorders are described as mild, moderate, or severe. Also like dyslexia, you may hear different names for each, but in all three cases, the brain functions differently than expected. Let's compare these disorders.

Comparison of Difficulties with Dyslexia, Dysgraphia, and Dyscalculia

DYSLEXIA

- Phonological awareness
- Accurately and fluently reading

Dyslexia and Dysgraphia:

- Spelling
- Handwriting

Dyslexia and Dyscalculia:

- Solving word problems
- Remembering math vocabulary

All three:

- Performing at grade level without intervention
- Standardized assessment

DYSGRAPHIA

- Written expression
- Writing legibly
- Writing speed
- Getting ideas down on paper

Dysgraphia and Dyscalculia:

- Writing numbers
- Organizing larger numbers for computations

DYSCALCULIA

- Understanding numbers
- Number-related concepts
- Using mathematical symbols and functions
- Mathematical computation

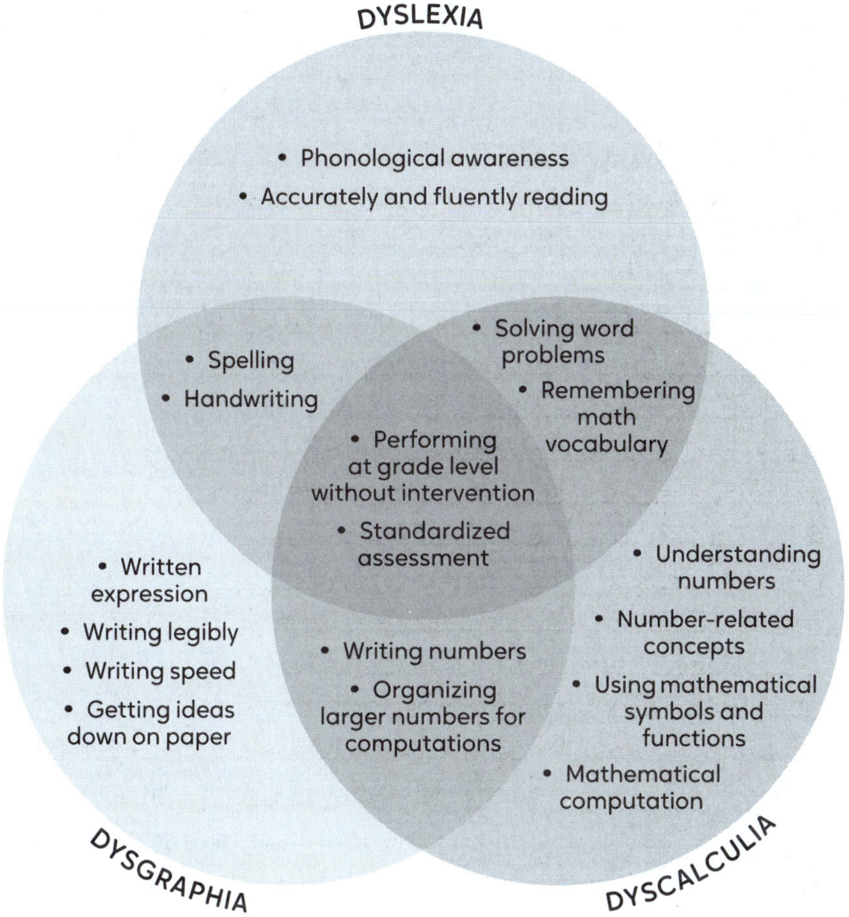

Neurodevelopmental Conditions That Are Not Learning Disorders

There are some disorders that, while not defined as learning differences, can affect how the brain grows and develops over time, especially during childhood. People with these neurodevelopmental disorders have brains that are wired differently, which can lead to differences in how a person thinks, learns, behaves, or interacts with others. Dyslexia is both neurobiological, because it is present at birth, and neurodevelopmental, because its symptoms appear as the child grows. It is also possible for someone with a diagnosis of dyslexia to receive a diagnosis of one or more other neurodevelopmental disorder(s).

The table below presents the typical characteristics of four neurodevelopmental disorders to help you understand their impacts.

Autism Spectrum Disorder (ASD)	Difficulty with social communication Restricted interests Repetitive behaviors Sensory sensitivities
Attention Deficit/ Hyperactivity Disorder (ADHD)	Impulsivity Inattention Hyperactivity Distractibility
Sensory Processing Disorder (SPD)	Difficulty processing and responding to sensory stimuli
Developmental Coordination Disorder (DCD), or Dyspraxia	Difficulty with motor coordination, planning, and execution

Language Disorders and Impairments

Several language disorders and impairments can coexist with dyslexia and may even make symptoms worse. The likelihood of an overlap is estimated to be 40 to 60 percent, and while that may sound alarming, early intervention helps here, too. To understand the impact language has on reading and writing, it's important to know the four domains of language and how they flow together:

1. Listening
2. Speaking
3. Reading
4. Writing

The figure shows how these four domains flow together.

A person can have difficulties with any of these domains. For some, a speech sound disorder (i.e., articulation disorder)

The Domains of Language

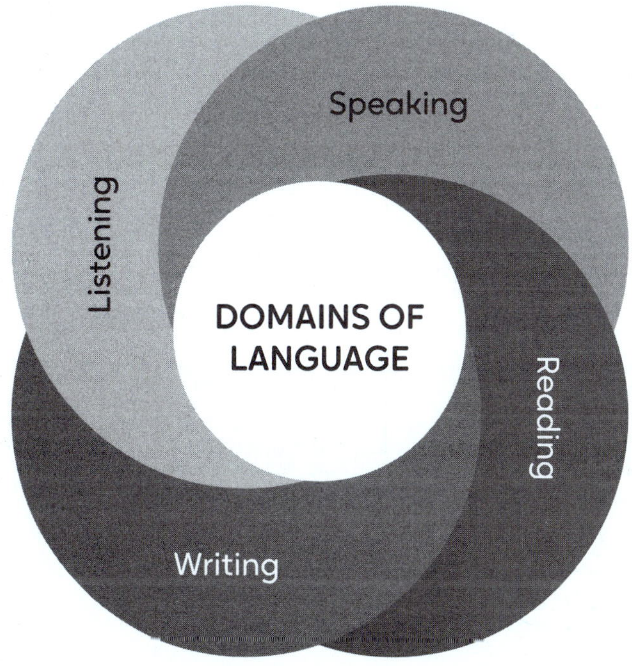

affects how someone produces the sounds in language. For example, a child may struggle to make the /l/ sound long after their peers.

Others may have difficulty understanding spoken language (receptive language disorder) or expressing themselves through speaking (expressive language disorder). There are also disorders that can impact language processing, grammar, social communication, and auditory processing. Listening and speaking skills underpin reading skills, so all these disorders can make dyslexia symptoms worse.

A person with a phonological disorder has difficulty understanding the rules for how sounds work in language. The child may delete sounds or syllables, like saying "nado" instead of "tornado." This is, in fact, an early red flag for dyslexia, as both are linked to phonological processing difficulties. This can easily be overlooked by parents, teachers, and even some speech pathologists, so it's understandable if this went unrecognized in your child.

Social and Emotional Concerns

Academic anxiety can be a common occurrence in a child with dyslexia. Fear of failure, stress, and persistent worry regarding their performance and social concerns in the school setting can be an issue for your child, even without a diagnosis of an anxiety disorder. Knowing you have to read in class when reading is really hard for you would make anyone anxious. A child with dyslexia may also experience depression, frustration, anger, sadness, and low self-esteem. We'll explore more about this in chapter 5.

Misdiagnoses

Dyslexia is just one reason a child might be struggling to read. Because there are multiple layers, diagnosing dyslexia is not always a straightforward process. Some children do get misdiagnosed. Though statistics vary, it's more common than you might expect. Reflect on everything you've learned so far. Is your child's reading struggle caused by word-level reading or do you think other factors are at play?

If you suspect your child was misdiagnosed, ask to see the full report and share it with another dyslexia specialist for a second opinion, if you can. You can compare the assessments used with information provided by the International Dyslexia Association about testing. You can also ask for a reevaluation and gather evidence to share with the dyslexia evaluator. The assessment process is complicated, but it's also important to listen to your instincts.

Before rushing ahead, though, weigh the benefits of a dyslexia diagnosis, such as access to services and accommodations, with the risk of being misdiagnosed. While you want to make sure your child receives the correct diagnosis, a dyslexia diagnosis could provide the reading intervention that your child needs given their identified struggles.

Who Treats Dyslexia and How?

Throughout this book, you'll often come across the words "interventionist," "intervention," and "classroom instruction." Depending on where you live, you may hear other similar but distinct terms. Generally speaking, when discussing your child's needs, these are some terms to know:

Types of Instruction

Classroom instruction: the high-quality, effective language and literacy instruction that every child should receive; in a general education setting, all students, including those with dyslexia, receive core reading instruction, also referred to as tier I instruction.

Dyslexia intervention: the high-quality, effective instruction a person with dyslexia needs to learn to read; this is targeted, evidence-based instruction provided to students who struggle with reading and may be referred to as tier II or III instruction in a school setting.

Dyslexia therapy: highly specialized, long-term, intensive, individualized intervention provided by credentialed professionals (can be a regional term).

Remediation: intensive, individualized instruction designed to close skill gaps, often occurring in addition to classroom instruction but typically within a school setting.

Dyslexia program: a structured program offering specialized reading instruction for someone with dyslexia, often created by research institutions, nonprofit organizations, or individual companies; often proprietary and require individuals to be trained prior to delivering the program.

Types of Instructors

Tutor: someone who provides small-group or one on-one teaching, who may or may not have specific training in dyslexia, often outside of a school setting.

Dyslexia interventionist: the person delivering the dyslexia intervention; a teacher of varying qualifications who delivers targeted, evidence-based instruction to struggling readers, often within a school or tiered system of support, or the system that identifies tiers II and III.

Dyslexia practitioner: a general term for someone trained to apply dyslexia intervention methods, often with training in a specific program but without a master's degree; may be within a school setting or as an outside professional.

Dyslexia specialist: a broad term for someone with expertise in dyslexia, likely with dyslexia training and/or training in a specific program; may or may not hold a master's degree or certification; may be within a school setting or as an outside professional.

Dyslexia therapist: a highly trained professional who provides intensive dyslexia intervention, with a master's degree and certification (can be a regional term); may be within a school setting but typically is an outside professional.

Common Intervention Approaches

The way educators should teach all children to read is generally the same; the key difference is the intensity. Some learners may need instruction that is more explicit or more multisensory, or they may need more opportunities for practice, but the writing system of the English language functions the same for everyone.

Unfortunately, some approaches, such as "whole language" or "balanced literacy," rely on the misguided belief that children just "soak up" reading and that learning to read occurs naturally, but evidence has proven that these approaches are ineffective. With these approaches, students are not taught how to break apart words to read them but instead are encouraged to use cues such as the picture in the book, their background knowledge, and the first letter of the word to guess what they think the word is. Reading isn't guessing! Reading is looking at *every* letter on the page to accurately read the word. If you'd like to learn more, check out the podcast *Sold a Story* by Emily Hanford and the book *The Knowledge Gap* by Natalie Wexler.

How written language functions is not obvious or intuitive for someone with dyslexia, so they need to be explicitly taught how our writing system works. A child with dyslexia needs specialized instruction, likely in small groups or one-on-one. They need an educator who is diagnostic, prescriptive, responsive, and adaptive. Just like a doctor might, a qualified professional uses assessments and observations to determine how your child is progressing. They'll prescribe the right programs and approaches, respond to how your child is receiving and retaining the information, and adapt to your child's rate of progress and preferences.

The reality is, your child's classroom teacher won't have the capacity for this. Even if your child is receiving the best classroom instruction possible, it won't be intense enough. Your child needs to receive intervention in addition to their classroom instruction. It's therefore essential to advocate for your child to receive specialized instruction as quickly and as often as possible. These are the types of resources that may be available:

Public schools: Every child who shows signs of dyslexia is eligible to receive an evaluation. According to the Individuals with Disabilities Education Act (IDEA), if dyslexia is diagnosed and the child is eligible to receive services, they are entitled to evidence-based intervention. Your child should have an individualized education program (IEP) outlining their goals and the supports and services they will receive.

Private or independent schools: Schools that do not receive federal funding are not required to provide dyslexia services but must be compliant with the Americans with Disabilities Act (ADA). Private and independent schools vary greatly in what they provide in the school setting to a student with dyslexia. This can range from nothing to specialized support for students with dyslexia. Typically, the school will not offer a formal evaluation or diagnosis. The family is often responsible for finding an outside professional to assess their child.

Outside of school: Check out the resources section on page 231 for a list of reliable websites. A range of professionals offer intervention services for dyslexia. Local nonprofits may be available to support families and learners.

If this feels like a lot, it's okay. I'll walk you through all of this as we proceed. Right now, take a moment to focus on the following:

- This will not be an easy journey, but it will be a successful one.

- You must advocate for your child.
- Be prepared to switch providers and fight for services.
- You're in this for the long haul. Your child will receive intervention services for a minimum of one to three years.
- Openly communicate with your child's teachers and service providers.
- Understand appropriate accommodations and how to ask for them.
- Trust your gut and get second opinions whenever necessary.

Intervention Program Methodology

All the best dyslexia intervention programs are based on the same methodology. This methodology has different names with slightly different meanings but are all basically the same:

- Structured literacy
- Science of reading
- Code-based instruction
- Phonics-based instruction
- The Orton-Gillingham (OG) approach

In the world of dyslexia, you'll hear about the Orton-Gillingham approach, which is the most commonly used. In the 1920s and '30s, Dr. Samuel Orton, a neuropsychiatrist, and Anna Gillingham, an educator and linguist, were the first people to develop a structured, multisensory approach to teaching reading, which became the foundation for dyslexia intervention programs. Any program based on this method refers to a systematic approach to teaching the skills required to learn to read and write. This is what you want for your child.

Your child's dyslexia intervention program should be:

Personalized: As Anna Gillingham said, "Go as fast as you can, but as slow as you must."

Systematic and sequential: Every piece of the learning-to-read puzzle is taught methodically and in order, based on evidence and research.

Explicit and direct: Your child is never asked to guess what they need to learn. They may investigate a topic but are told what they need to know at each step.

Structured and process-oriented: The building blocks of the language are taught layer by layer. Consistent procedures are taught so that your child can apply them independently.

Cumulative: Learning builds on itself and the connections are made clear for your child.

Intensive: Experts suggest that one-hour sessions, ideally four to five times a week, are ideal for significant progress.

Multisensory: The auditory, kinesthetic, tactile, and visual senses are used during learning. The more parts of the brain that work together, the stronger the connections will be.

Synthetic and analytic instruction: Your child will learn to break apart sounds to read and spell words (synthetic) and recognize word patterns to read and spell words (analytic).

Choosing the right program is partly finding the right fit and partly trial and error. The best programs delivered by a trained professional will help every child, but some programs may only be a good fit for some children. In addition, schools and professionals often already have a program in place, so you may not have a choice in which program your child receives. The best combination is a high-quality program and a well-trained professional. Thankfully, all the OG approach–based programs I mention will help your child.

Let's take a look at some OG approach–based trainings and programs:

- Alphabetic Phonics
- Barton Reading & Spelling System
- Neuhaus Education Center's Basic Language Skills
- Region 4 Education Service Center's Reading by Design
- Scottish Rite for Children's Take Flight
- Wilson Reading System

Notable OG-based programs intended for classroom or homeschool use include:

- 95 Percent Group's Phonics Core Program
- All About Reading
- Voyager Sopris Learning's LANGUAGE!
- The Slingerland Approach
- The Spalding Method
- Wilson's Fundations

While OG-based approaches are universally recognized as effective for learners with dyslexia, certain other approaches can be helpful when taught alongside an OG-based structured curriculum. For example, the Structured Word Inquiry approach explores the meaning, structure, and history of words and teaches word parts and how words are connected, while the Davis Dyslexia Program and Montessori approaches incorporate kinesthetic teaching. All three of these methods can benefit children who are being taught with OG-based approaches.

2

Their World through Dyslexia

The knowledge you've gained so far can help you better understand your child. If you had similar experiences in childhood, some of this may sound familiar, but perhaps it's all new to you. Regardless of your own experiences, your child's world is unique, so trust your parental instincts and don't feel as if you're overreacting. To help you conceptualize what it is like for your child, this chapter introduces two fictional scenarios based on real-life children with dyslexia. Of course, the best way to understand your child is to watch, ask, and listen.

Your Child's Experience

Dyslexia will undoubtedly impact your child's experience of the world. School will likely be difficult, but amazing possibilities exist outside the classroom. Fortunately, your child's dyslexia was identified early, and they are about to receive or have started receiving the right support. Not only have you already made some impactful first steps, but reading this book gives you and your child the advantage of knowledge and preparation. This is wonderful because your child's brain is still developing and can adapt and learn. Change *is* possible, and your child's future is bright.

Academically, your biggest role now is to support and advocate for your child:

- Ensure they receive explicit, structured, multisensory instruction.
- Build in ample time for them to practice reading skills.
- Provide them with helpful tools and strategies at home.
- Be their emotional rock when they need it.
- Foster and reinforce their strengths and talents.

Your child's future may look different from what you once imagined for them—but they are on the right track and so are you!

Your Child at School

Let's take a walk through a typical school day for a child with dyslexia. Emma is in second grade at a public school. Recently diagnosed, she's relieved to understand that her brain learns differently, making reading hard.

Emma starts her school day chatting with friends—one of her favorite parts of the day because there's nothing to read! She walks in and her teacher, Mrs. Lopez, greets her. It's time for math, which Emma loves—except for word problems; those are tough.

After math, Mr. Smith, Emma's dyslexia interventionist, takes her to another classroom. Emma's sad to miss art, music, and PE, but she's also excited because Mr. Smith teaches her how to read and builds in time to practice. It's hard, but she's improving. She read her first book last week!

Thankfully, after all that work, it's recess. Moving her body helps her feel relaxed and ready to learn again. Afterward, Emma is back in her classroom—it's time for reading. She fidgets and glances around. Everyone else is reading, but Emma only pretends. She knows how to read Mr. Smith's materials, so why is reading still so hard?

Emma remembers her bathroom pass—a momentary escape. When she returns, her group is at Mrs. Lopez's table. Mrs. Lopez uses the stories and resources Emma learned with Mr. Smith to help her keep practicing. The other kids sometimes laugh when Emma stumbles while reading, and Mrs. Lopez scolds them, but she still feels bad.

Another favorite part of the school day is at the end, when she has basketball practice. When she gets home, she's glad the only book she'll see is the one her dad reads to her at bedtime. That's her absolute favorite part of the day!

Emma's story may be similar to what your child experiences during an average school day. Keep her story in mind as you continue.

Other Areas of Development

Let's look at some common difficulties in other developmental areas your child may be struggling in. If any of this sounds like what your child is experiencing and they have not been evaluated in these areas, contact your child's school or speak with a specialist.

Cognitive and Other Academic Skills

Dyslexia is a language-based learning disorder, so we know that other disorders involving language processing, rapid naming, and word retrieval difficulties can be more common for someone with dyslexia. This means your child may need more time to understand what they hear or read. They may struggle to find the right word at times, using general terms like "thing" or "that" instead of something more specific during ordinary conversations.

Other cognitive functions may also be at play, such as working memory, processing speed, and executive functioning skills. While we can look at these as separate skills, they are interrelated. A strength in one boosts the rest, while a deficit in one compounds issues in the others. This can feel like a chicken-or-egg scenario, so it's important for a qualified professional to determine the root cause or causes of your child's difficulties and suggest appropriate supplementary supports.

Let's look at these three cognitive functions a little more closely:

Working memory: The ability to hold and manipulate information over short periods. It's the brain's whiteboard (e.g., remembering ingredients for a recipe as you prepare to make it). This differs from long-term memory, which is the almost limitless information our brains can store, and short-term memory, which is information we hold on to that we're currently processing; we can typically hold on to around seven things for 20 to 30 seconds.

Processing speed: How quickly the brain takes in, understands, and responds to information (e.g., a timed trivia game).

Executive functioning skills: These form the brain's "control center," which helps us plan, organize, make decisions, stay focused, and solve problems (e.g., planning and packing for a trip).

The diagram below shows the roles and overlap of these three cognitive functions to help you visualize potential difficulties.

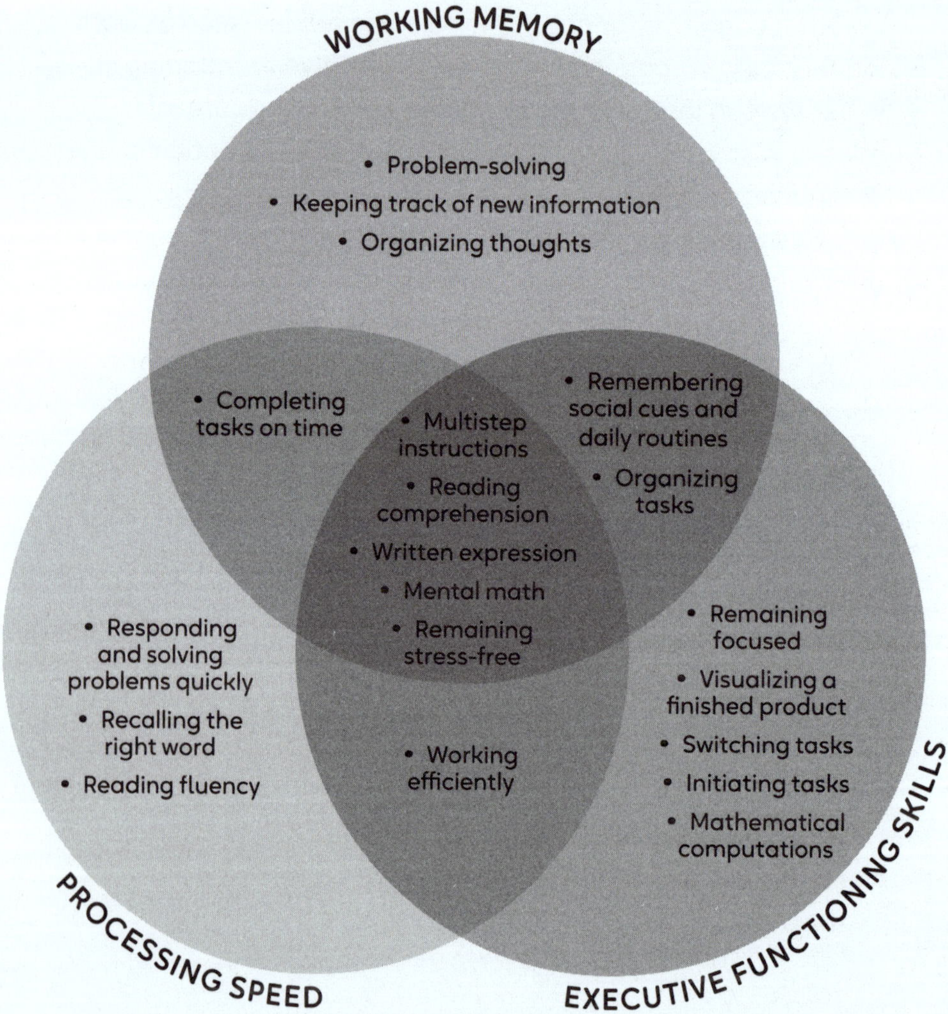

Sensory and Motor Integration: The Link between Body and Brain

Not every person with dyslexia has sensory and motor difficulties, but it isn't uncommon. Sensory integration difficulties refer to challenges in processing and responding to sensory input, such as what you hear, see, or feel. If this is a challenge for your child, this can affect how they interact with the world—for example:

Auditory (Hearing)

- Finds it harder to understand someone in loud places.
- Has difficulty focusing in noisy classrooms.

Visual (Sight)

- Skips lines when reading.
- Winces at bright lights.
- Experiences headaches or eyestrain after reading or focusing.

Tactile (Touch)

- Finds certain types of fabric or clothes uncomfortable.
- Experiences hand fatigue after writing for an extended period.

The brain tells the body how to move in order for us to complete an action using small muscle movements (fine motor skills) and big muscle movements (gross motor skills). In chapter 7, we'll talk more about these areas of development and why it's important to understand them for your child with dyslexia. Motor coordination difficulties are not related to reading struggles in dyslexia; however, for educational purposes, here are a few examples of what these challenges may look like:

Fine Motor Challenges

- Messy handwriting
- Has difficulty tying shoelaces or cutting with scissors

Gross Motor Challenges

- Struggles to ride a bike or complete tasks that require balance
- Frequently trips or stumbles
- Struggles to catch or throw a ball

Social and Emotional Development

Dyslexia is not a social/emotional disorder, but you may have noticed that your child's interactions with their peers and friends have changed or the way they feel about themselves is different. Maybe you've seen them be self-conscious or exhibit sensitive reactions. Anxiety and frustration can lead to big emotions, which your child may not yet have the maturity to regulate. Socially speaking, some children with dyslexia (with or without coexisting challenges) may, unfortunately, be the target of teasing or bullying. We'll discuss this more in chapter 5.

Strengths and Gifts

During your journey, you'll discover *many* ways to help your child learn to meet their challenges. But it's also essential to allow your child to recognize and build on their strengths and gifts so that they have opportunities to feel successful and be a leader. You know your child so well, including which activities, sports, hobbies, and/or extracurricular activities build their confidence and let them truly shine. What follows on page 48 are some other ways to explore your child's talents.

Technology and Assistive Accommodations

"Accommodations" refer to the changes a school can put in place with regard to the learning environment and the teaching approach. So the classroom's setup or a teacher's methods or assessments can change, but not the educational content.

Your child with dyslexia will benefit from both technological and non-tech accommodations. Keep in mind, though, that not all children will prefer to use technology and some learners with dyslexia may actually find technology distracting or more difficult to manage. To give you an idea of what your child may be using in school, here are some common accommodations:

Non-Tech Accommodations

- Alternative assignments like oral presentations or creating a poster
- Extended time
- Reduced reading material
- Shortened writing tasks
- Slant boards
- Special writing implements such as chunky pencils or writing grips

Tech Accommodations

- Using a keyboard for writing assignments
- Spell-check
- Apps or extensions
- Audiobooks
- Speech-to-text and text-to-speech technology

- Team sports are a great way to build social skills, make connections, and constructively burn off extra energy.
- Some children with dyslexia are incredible orators and thrive in theater and other performing arts.
- Some children with dyslexia may prefer more solitary creative hobbies like playing a musical instrument, doing puzzles, painting, making ceramics, sewing, or gardening. These can also help a child develop fine motor skills.

Although a dyslexia diagnosis means your child primarily struggles with decoding, it doesn't mean they lack strengths in other areas. In fact, the Sea of Strengths model, developed by Dr. Sally Shaywitz, emphasizes the many areas where children with dyslexia may shine.

Sea of Strengths Model

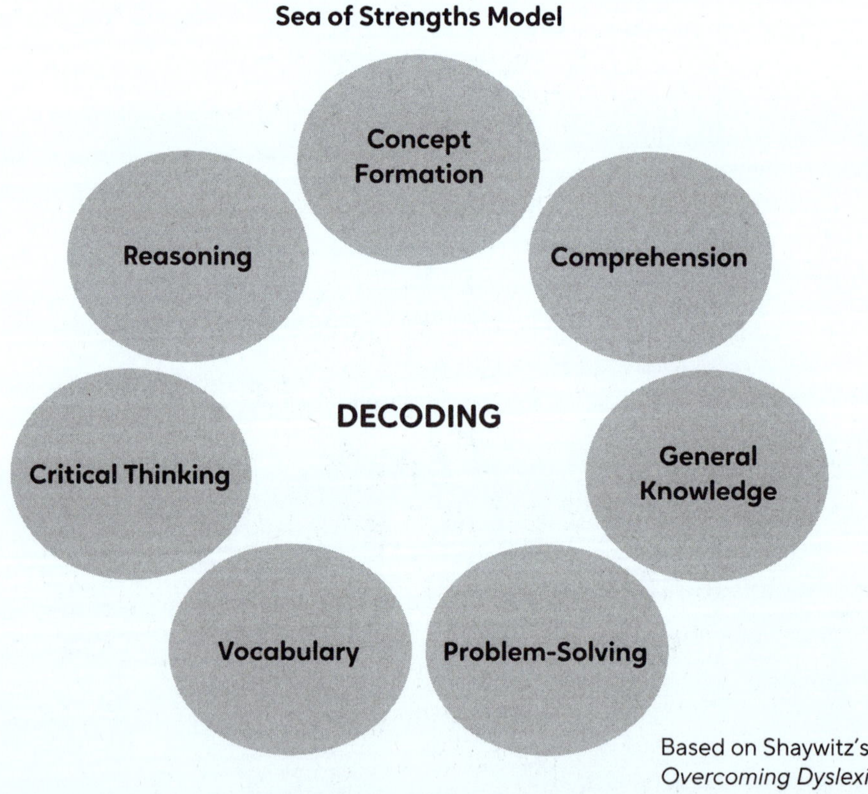

Based on Shaywitz's *Overcoming Dyslexia*

Precisely because there is a "sea of strengths," you may hear that "dyslexia is a superpower." However, Dr. Timothy Odegard, an expert in dyslexia research, cautions against stereotyping. Some children may not think of their dyslexia as a superpower, so ask your child what they think. If this slogan resonates, use it! If it does, I recommend *The Dyslexic Advantage* by Drs. Brock and Fernette Eide. If it doesn't, that's okay, too.

Embrace your child's interests and strengths as opportunities to honor their talents, overcome their challenges, celebrate their wins, and build essential life skills to help them champion for themselves.

Talking about Dyslexia

Maybe you haven't told your child about their diagnosis yet and you aren't sure how to approach the topic—or even if you want to. That was the case for private school third-grader Abi's mom. Abi felt smart but found reading hard. When the school year ended, Abi's mom, Sharon, took him to a psychologist but did not tell Abi why. She seemed nervous, so Abi figured he should be, too.

A month later, Sharon received the psychologist's report, in which Abi was diagnosed with dyslexia. When Sharon shared this information with her co-parent, they discussed the stigma surrounding dyslexia and decided not to tell Abi to "keep him from feeling dumb." They weren't sure they wanted the school to know, either.

That summer, Abi started dyslexia intervention with Ms. Lu, who found him to be incredibly intelligent; he just needed someone to teach him in a way that made sense for his brain. Abi's reading accelerated, but Ms. Lu suggested to Sharon that telling the school—and Abi—would be in his best interest. Sharon and her co-parent still decided against it.

The new school year started better for Abi because he could read what he was supposed to, but he didn't understand why he still found new lessons so hard. Abi felt dumb, which is exactly what his parents didn't want. When they realized Abi was no longer excited to go to school and had even started to avoid hanging out with friends outside of school, they decided to share his diagnosis with him. Abi finally understood why some tasks at school were hard; his brain just worked a little differently. Fast-forward, and Abi is now an empowered middle schooler who confidently advocates for his needs. He understands what dyslexia means for him and knows helpful tools and strategies.

Talking with your child about their dyslexia diagnosis may feel like a big hurdle, but here are a few scripts to help you get started.

Chances are you've already navigated the diagnosis process and can see the light at the end of the tunnel, but if not, here's a script you can use or adapt to help your child better understand the assessment process:

> "We are going to (*name the type of place*) to meet (*name the doctor or specialist*). This is an expert who will help us understand *how* you learn. They are going to ask you to look at pictures of shapes, read words, and talk about what you see or know. It's okay if you don't know the answers. You can say you're not sure."

If you haven't yet shared your child's diagnosis of dyslexia with them, try this script, but first, make sure your child is ready for this news and isn't distracted by anything. Find a quiet time to sit down together.

> "Do you remember meeting (*name the doctor*)? We talked about how they would help us understand how you learn. We want to share what (*the doctor*) discovered about how special your brain is and how it works when you're trying to read."
>
> "We know sometimes reading can be tricky for you even though you're so smart and try so hard, but it's not your fault. Your brain just works differently. You have something called dyslexia, which means you'll be able to work with a special teacher to learn how to read and spell."

While it may feel uncomfortable, sharing your child's diagnosis with people outside your family can help strengthen relationships and build community. Aside from your child and your child's school and teacher, here's a list of people to tell:

- Immediate family
- Health-care providers
- Interventionist and other professionals

After a thoughtful discussion, here's a list of people you might consider telling:

- Extended family
- Your child's close friends
- Support groups and other parents
- Close friends and your social network

3

Supporting Your Child's Journey

You probably noticed that your child's diagnosis has changed not only their version of reality but also yours—or at least what you thought life would look like moving forward. This may cause some fear and anxiety but also hope that your child will be equipped with the tools they need to thrive. In this process, your child will learn and grow, but so will you. You are embarking on a unique but parallel experience with your child as they learn with dyslexia. I encourage you to remember that your experience may be similar to other parents', but it is also unique to you, your child, and your family. Dyslexia is not a phase to grow out of, but a journey that will change over time as your child grows. This chapter is all about paving a path toward sustainable practices that will carry you, your family, and your child into a positive future.

Fostering Support and Building Relationships

Now that you have answers to why your child struggles with reading, know that this diagnosis doesn't define them or you, but it will take time for you to grow into your new role as a parent or caregiver of a child with dyslexia. With the information and strategies from this book, you are in the driver's seat now, but not forever. Your child will eventually have to take over, and this is your chance to show them how to do it. You have an empowering opportunity to help your child develop their own agency. This is a new set of muscles that will take time to develop, so give yourself the grace and space to grow and learn with your child.

Your child has not changed, but your understanding of them has. You may even find that this new understanding has improved your relationship. Let this new knowledge transform your perspective of your child and adapt your role as their caretaker. Work to understand, listen to, and meet their struggles and needs as they grow and evolve, and continually seek to expand your tool kit of strategies. Reading this book means you're already on this path!

Your deeper understanding of your child gives you the chance to further nurture the beautiful relationship you share with them. Set aside special times together to strengthen your bond. Your child needs to know you're in their corner. Children usually remember the little things, so take advantage of small moments—a secret handshake, weekly trips to the park, baking cookies, building a pillow fort, or snuggling with a book all build lasting memories that shape a family.

More than ever, you'll need to be your child's emotional rock. You can help them understand their struggles and find their passions and their voice. You also must be prepared to defend your child's right to services and their basic human right to literacy. I cannot emphasize enough the importance of being your child's advocate during these crucial elementary school years. Be cautioned that the school may not always offer everything they're supposed to. I have worked with some parents who ultimately felt it necessary to sue their child's school. While I hope you never have to experience this, be prepared to fight for your child.

Your child with dyslexia is fortunate that the cause of their reading struggles was identified early. Yes, they are one of the lucky ones, as strange as that might sound. Along with your help and dedication, they can receive the right intervention and support. They will successfully learn to read—and may even develop a love of reading!

Daily Life at Home

We all know that a healthy lifestyle and consistency are important for children, but this can be even more true for your child with dyslexia. You may already be experiencing this, but your child will likely need intentional, additional support at home to complete schoolwork and integrate what they are learning in services received. If your child is managing multiple conditions, routines and mealtimes may prove challenging. Frustration and anxiety may stem from your child's reading struggles, so the stability that comes from a nurturing home life may play a larger role in supporting your child.

Part II looks more closely at specific strategies, but let's discuss the big picture now.

Healthy Habits

Building healthy habits sets any child up for a bright future. Be consistent about providing regular nutritious meals and minimizing processed foods and sugary snacks to avoid spikes and crashes, especially in children who have difficulty regulating their emotions. A growing body of scientific evidence states that omega-3 fatty acids and certain micronutrients such as zinc, iron, magnesium, and B vitamins may help brain function.

Follow your gut instincts to supplement your child's diet, and check with your child's pediatrician before making any major diet changes.

In addition to what they eat, the process of eating can be difficult for some children. Mealtimes can be challenging, especially if your child with dyslexia also has sensory integration issues, executive functioning deficits, or ADHD. Food may not interest them, they may be too distracted to sit and eat, certain medications may suppress their appetite, they may not realize they're hungry, or some smells or textures may be off-putting. We'll look at specific strategies in chapter 7, but if you feel that getting your child to eat is a battle, reach out to your pediatrician or a nutritionist, speech therapist, or other professional for extra help. Here are some additional tips:

- Create a consistent schedule around mealtimes and snack time.
- Preview meal choices with your child earlier in the week, if possible.
- Let your child take ownership over the eating process by having them help with grocery shopping and meal preparation, when possible.
- Tasty kid-safe protein shakes can ensure your child is getting the nutrients they need.

A healthy diet is key, and sleep is also an essential factor in your child's development. You may have heard that eight hours of sleep is sufficient, but children ages six to nine need nine to eleven hours of sleep. Here are some additional tips:

- A consistent bedtime will help your child maintain a healthy sleep schedule.

- Avoid screens during the few hours leading up to bedtime.
- Help your child unwind before bedtime with a relaxing activity.

Regular exercise will also help your child's overall health and can provide the release of endorphins and serotonin your child may need to reduce any feelings of anxiety related to academic tasks. Here are a few ideas to help with sensory and emotional regulation:

- Limit your child's screentime to an hour a day and do something more active together.
- Encourage your child to get at least an hour of physical activity a day.
- Let your child take the lead and show you a new workout or teach you a new dance.
- Incorporate structured and unstructured opportunities for movement.

Consistency, Routines, and Rewards

Everyday life can understandably sometimes force us to break routines, but aiming for consistency in your child's day-to-day can help diminish the need for prompts, reminders, and even fights. When your child knows what to expect and when, it helps them move more easily through their day.

Remember, school will likely be a big challenge for your child, so the more you can do to help them know what to expect, the more brain power they will have to dive into their intervention program. We'll look at specific strategies in chapters 5 and 6 to build routines and structure into your child's day.

In addition to regular mealtimes, consider prioritizing consistency in these areas:

- Morning, after-school, and bedtime routines
- Materials and preparation for school
- Quiet place to practice and complete homework
- Unstructured downtime

You may find it necessary to incorporate a positive reward system into your child's routines to keep them motivated. While the idea is to diminish the need for incentives as much as possible, a reward system may be the stepping stone your child needs to build independence. If you are considering using a reward chart:

- Be clear with your child about the expectations.
- Always focus on the positive.
- Never take away an earned reward.
- Be consistent.
- Let your child feel like they're part of the process by setting their own goals and choosing their own reasonable reward.

Cues and Redirections

Children between the ages of six and nine need reminders to successfully navigate their day. Because their brains continue to develop into their 20s, your child's working memory, impulse control, and emotion regulation skills are still works in progress. For a child with dyslexia and possibly other cognitive differences, this developmental process may be slower than expected.

Be prepared to provide cues and redirections to help your child stay on task. Chapter 5 looks at strategies related to social/emotional development, but here are a few tips to help your child complete essential daily tasks successfully and increasingly independently:

- Nonverbal communication is a great way to cue your child without overwhelming their language processing. For example, mutually understood hand gestures can remind your child to put on their shoes or pack their backpack. These can be an opportunity to let your child have fun and develop some "secret spy signals."
- Using your child's favorite song can help keep them on track during daily routines like getting ready for school. Talk with your child about what needs to be done during the song and then leave them to the task. You may tire of the song, but it might be the trick needed to help your child complete a routine.
- Completing tasks with your child is another great way to cue them. For example, brush your teeth alongside your child.

Managing Multiple Conditions

A child with dyslexia needs to receive intensive, structured, explicit, multisensory intervention, likely for a minimum of three hours a week. Depending on your child's school, this may not be possible during the school day. If that's the case, consider seeking services that take place after school and/or on weekends. This intensity might diminish as your child moves through their intervention program; regardless, they'll need to receive these services throughout their academic journey.

Finding time for everything may prove challenging, especially if your child is managing multiple conditions. Here are a few ideas to keep your child's schedule from feeling overwhelming:

- Work closely with your child's team to determine the best schedule for your child.
- If you're balancing services for multiple conditions, use school holidays for booster courses.
- Take advantage of summer break. Some of the best learning can happen when your child is not tired from long school days.

While school holidays and summer vacation are intended as breaks, and your child should have downtime to recharge and absorb what they've learned, extended breaks can negatively impact your child's rate of progress. When school is not in session, find the right balance between relaxing and learning.

Reinforce the learning that's happening at school and in your child's intervention or therapy sessions. This may look different depending on the services your child receives. Regardless of your child's goals, there are exciting ways to apply their learning at home without making it feel like work. You'll find lots of strategies in part II, but here are some ideas to make the most of their at-home learning time:

- The more time your child has to practice reading, including repeated readings of the same words or texts, the more quickly they can build new skills. Building in quiet, daily reading practice is key. Communicate with your child's dyslexia interventionist so you have the same or similar materials at home. Also, your child's listening comprehension skills will be significantly more advanced than their reading comprehension skills for many years, so continue to read aloud to your child, even as they get older.

- A child with dyslexia who has coexisting conditions may also receive other therapies, such as play, occupational, or speech. Communicate with your child's team about their goals and find fun ways to practice the skills learned. Playgrounds are a great place for your child to practice social interactions and build gross motor skills. Many children with sensory integration issues love monkey bars and swings, which provide the sensory input they're seeking.
- Playdates and family outings are good opportunities for your child to build social and pragmatic language skills.
- Sewing, cutting, coloring, building something, and helping to cook are all fun ways to develop fine motor skills.
- For a child who also has eating challenges, gamifying mealtimes can help them apply what they've learned in speech therapy sessions about chewing and swallowing.

Fostering Attunement

Now that you've had time to sit with your child's diagnosis, you may be feeling grief and guilt, shock and denial, and/or stress and anxiety. You may be concerned about navigating new systems, acquiring access to services, or juggling insurance and financial strains. All of this is expected and understandable. Reflect on your feelings, whatever they may be. The better you understand yourself, the better you can connect with your child and model ways to cope with stress.

A big part of life has changed for your child. I promise, though, it's changed for the better. You'll want to respond to your child in ways that show you are aware that life may feel different now that you understand them, are sensitive to their needs, are willing to help, and will accept whatever feelings they may be having. In addition, be sure to:

- Celebrate and value your child's efforts, not just the progress being made.
- Be your child's cheerleader, regardless of the outcome.
- Keep track of their progress in their intervention program and celebrate the milestones.
- Be aware of your child's natural pace and avoid overly pressuring them to perform.
- Allow your child to stumble at times to give them the opportunity to overcome challenges by themselves and build resilience.

On these last two points, think of children as trees. Some grow faster than others, and some will be taller or stouter than others. They all grow at their own pace, but they grow best in nutritious soil with just the right amount of water and sun.

Trees also need wind. They need to be pushed and tested by changing, buffeting winds. This is how they grow strong roots and trunks to weather storms. Resistance builds resilience. Only you know how to find that delicate balance between supporting and stepping back. That said, there are some burdens a child should *never* carry alone, including:

- Physical pain
- Emotional struggles

- Social/emotional concerns
- Misunderstandings with friends or family
- Academic challenges outside your child's comfort zone of learning
- Any situation that just feels too big for your child

A Balanced and Nourished Life for You and Your Child

Supporting your child with dyslexia means putting yourself first when you need to. If you're not balanced, nourished, and regulated, it makes it very hard for you to be those things for your child. Healthy habits not only sustain you but also help you model a balanced lifestyle for your child that they can use throughout their life. Make sure you find quiet times to recharge, self-care routines to relax, and grounding exercises to regulate and rebalance. You may find it helpful to socialize with friends and family or find local support groups. Try local branches of the International Dyslexia Association or Decoding Dyslexia, both of which can be found through the International Dyslexia Association website. Find what works for you, and be flexible and change as you need to.

Parents and caregivers of any child feel the pressures of unrealistic expectations in today's world. Through technology and social media, parents may feel more empowered to be actively engaged in the lives of their children. However, remember it can also build pressure and distort what realistic expectations look like. Doing everything "just right" can cause stress, burnout, and guilt. You're doing the best you can—and that's what your child needs. The more we embrace failure as

Practical Tips for Emotional Attunement

- **Use play to express emotions.** Kids often show their emotions through play rather than talking about them. Try different activities like drawing, storytelling, or imaginative play to encourage your child to share how they're feeling.
- **Talk about examples of feelings.** Identify emotions that come up in books or movies and ask your child questions about it. "How do you think they feel? Have you ever felt that way?" You can use your own small moments to model this as well.
- **Check in regularly.** Use routine moments like bedtime, car rides, or waiting in line to share how you're feeling and encourage your child to do the same.
- **Reflect their feelings.** Instead of rushing in to make your child feel better, simply acknowledge how they're feeling. "It sounds like you felt really left out when that happened."
- **Encourage "I feel" statements.** Help them express emotions clearly with statements like, "I feel (emotion) when (situation) because (reason)."
- **Foster open communication with questions,** such as:
    - "What was the silliest thing that happened today?"
    - "What made you feel happy today?"
    - "Who did you play with today? What did you like about what you did together?"
    - "If something was bothering you at school, who would you talk to?"
    - "Can you show me with your face how you felt today?" (Model a happy face, a worried face, etc.)

learning opportunities, the better we are at navigating bumps in the road.

Psychologist Carol Dweck first introduced the concept of a growth mindset in her 2006 book *Mindset: The New Psychology of Success*. In her research, Dweck discovered that people's beliefs about their abilities and intelligence, whether they are fixed or growth-oriented, can significantly affect how they approach challenges and setbacks in life. Embracing a growth mindset for you and your child can be an anchor in this walk. Helping your child understand and experience firsthand that their efforts will have an impact on their abilities will fuel their resilience and motivation. When you are encouraging a growth mindset in both you and your child, remember to:

- Praise effort, not just abilities or achievements.
- Emphasize the opportunities that challenges present.
- Normalize mistakes and failures as simply first attempts.
- Embrace the power of "yet" (a mindset to keep trying).

The World around You and Your Child

With what we've covered so far, you now have a better understanding of your child's struggles and how to provide support, praise their efforts, and celebrate their wins—but you don't have to do it alone. Professionals who are trained in dyslexia are ready to help you and your child. It's key to recognize when it's time to seek help, so let's look at the network of services you may need to consider at some point and the best practices for keeping services ongoing.

Building Your Child's Team within the Network of Services

Part of your job is to ensure that your child receives *what* they need *when* they need it. This requires advocating and communicating. Your first stop for questions regarding dyslexia-specific services should be your child's school. Ideally, someone there can support you and help you navigate the network of services. In cases where certain services are not available within the school setting, you may need to seek the help of an outside professional.

For dyslexia intervention to be as effective as possible, your child's team should communicate with each other. The more consistency there is with approaches and across settings, the more effective intervention will be. Be ready for a few logistics, though:

- If your child is receiving services outside of school, it's up to you to connect those professionals with your child's teacher. In order to speak with your child's teacher, a quality interventionist will ask you to sign a confidentiality release.
- In some cases, it may fall on you to share reports and updates.
- Use technology to alleviate some of the woes of coordinating. Take advantage of shared calendars, collaborative notes, and other ways to communicate across a team.

Let's look at the types of professionals your child may need for support at different points in their journey.

Must Have

- Dyslexia interventionist*
- Evaluator*
- Pediatrician

Might Need (depends on coexisting conditions)

- Speech language pathologist*
- Occupational therapist*
- Play therapist
- Physical therapist
- Counselor or psychologist*
- Psychiatrist
- Developmental, behavioral, or occupational optometrist

*May be available through your child's school.

If your child is receiving services outside of school, you may find scheduling all their appointments challenging. Because high-quality professionals are so sought after, they often have limited availability or even waitlists. Make the soonest appointment you can, as there are important developmental cognitive windows during which therapy and intervention are much more effective. Be prepared to make difficult decisions like missing out on other activities to ensure your child receives the best support possible at the right time.

This level of intervention won't last forever. In the beginning, your child's schedule may feel overwhelming. You can work closely with your child's team to create a balanced schedule that works for your family.

Speak with your child's providers about how long a program might last. A good interventionist cannot make promises, but after getting to know your child, they will be able to speak to their current rate of progress and goals. Your child's interventionist, as well as their school and classroom teacher, can join the conversation in knowing what to prioritize when. A high-quality intervention program is essential, but it may be possible to layer in other services over the summer or later on depending on what your child needs. Based on this, members of your child's team might be able to give you a possible projected timeline. Be prepared for this to change as your child's needs change.

Let's use a real-world example to see what your child's schedule might look like below. Jose is seven years old and has been diagnosed with dyslexia, social language difficulties, and ADHD. He is receiving a high-quality, effective dyslexia intervention program four times a week during school, but his parents know he needs additional support for his other challenges. They have worked hard to find low-cost options and are grateful their insurance will cover six months of speech therapy.

Monday	Speech therapy to build Jose's language skills (duration: six months)
Wednesday	Occupational therapy to help Jose regulate his sensory input and manage impulsivity (duration: ongoing)
Friday	Play therapy to help Jose manage his big emotions and understand the reasons for his struggles with reading (duration: three months)
Saturday	Weekly swim lessons at the public pool so that Jose can make friends in a supportive, structured environment that gives him a chance to be successful (duration: ongoing)
School vacations	Social language camp to help him practice his skills from speech therapy in group settings Soccer camp because Jose loves the sport

Finding the Right Professionals

The world of dyslexia services can feel like the Wild West because there are multiple credentialing organizations. The table on page 69 clarifies some of the titles and credentials you may come across in your search. This information is not specific to any state, which may have their own board of education or licensing body for teachers.

Always choose a credentialed or licensed professional with experience. This is a lot of information to take in, so just breathe through it! Don't be afraid to ask questions and get them answered to your satisfaction. Some questions you may consider asking include:

- What is their experience, training, and credentials? Did they receive a certification of completion or are they fully credentialed or licensed?
- What programs do they use? How effective are these programs?
- How will they assess your child's initial skill levels and their progress throughout the program?
- How will they set goals for your child?
- How can they adapt the program based on your child's needs?
- How often can you expect communication from them, such as phone calls, emails, and progress reports?
- How will they get to know your child?
- How will they communicate with your child about their progress?

Organization	Credential	Degree Required
Academic Language Therapy Association (ALTA)*	Certified Academic Language Practitioner (CALP)	Bachelor's
	Certified Academic Language Therapist (CALT)	Master's
Center for Effective Reading Instruction (CERI)**	Certified Structured Literacy/ Dyslexia Interventionist	Bachelor's
	Certified Structured Literacy/ Dyslexia Specialist	Bachelor's
Academy of Orton-Gillingham Practitioners and Educators (AOGPE)**	AOGPE Certified Level	Bachelor's
	AOGPE Fellow Level	Master's
Wilson Language Training**	Wilson Level I Certification/ Practitioner	Bachelor's
	Wilson Level II Certification/ Therapist	Bachelor's

*This organization credentials professionals from accredited programs and training centers.

**This organization credentials professionals who have completed their own proprietary trainings.

Setting Goals and Keeping Track of Progress

You should always have front-row access to the goals that have been set for your child's intervention program and to the information you need to keep track of their progress. Learning to read is like building a skyscraper. The skills your child is taught need to be developed in the correct order. Because of this, every dyslexia intervention program has a scope and sequence, or a preset order of concepts for a child to learn. The program may be broken up into units, volumes, or books, but every topic your child's interventionist will teach them is in a certain order for logical reasons. For example, your child will learn that the letter "T" makes the /t/ sound before they learn about "th."

A high-quality program includes explicit instruction across every level of the language as well as practice with speaking and listening skills. At minimum, your child's intervention program will incorporate all the letter/sound correspondences.

Because the intervention program will be tailored to your child, always ask the interventionist what you should expect and how you'll be able to gauge improvement at home. Check in with your child from time to time as well as with the interventionist on a regular basis to be sure your child is progressing as expected.

While consistency in the program is essential for your child's progress, a time may come when it's necessary to make a change. Here are some signs it might be time to look for another interventionist:

- If you don't feel a solid connection/relationship with the interventionist after one month
- If your child's personality and the interventionist's personality aren't a good fit

- If your child's attitude about sessions or reading deteriorates at any point
- If you are not seeing progress after six months

Navigating the School System

Navigating your child's school system may seem overwhelming at times, but as with everything, knowledge is power. This process may seem extra confusing, as every school is a little different. The main factors to note are where the school is located and if they receive federal funding.

If your child attends a school that receives federal funding here in the United States, there are legal requirements in place. The Individuals with Disabilities Education Act (IDEA), Section 504 of the Rehabilitation Act (Section 504), and the Americans with Disabilities Act (ADA) all ensure that your child receives an appropriate education that meets their needs. IDEA ensures that your child is eligible for special education services. Dyslexia is explicitly listed as a disability under this law.

Remember that "disability" is the legal term for a specific learning disorder. This means that if your child is showing signs of dyslexia, then, legally, they must be evaluated to determine whether they qualify for a diagnosis.

If your child hasn't been evaluated yet, don't let the school provide tier II instruction as part of their multi-tiered system of support (MTSS) or response to intervention (RTI) system in lieu of assessing your child. Every school is different, but some schools may be motivated to provide support instead of a diagnosis. Either they're following outdated methods of determining eligibility that wait for a child to fail before diagnosing, or they may simply not have the resources to diagnose your child, even though they should.

If you hear a school using the terms MTSS or RTI, but not discussing an evaluation, then be wary. Each state calls it something different, but you should hear the terms "full and individual evaluation" or "initial evaluation." Advocate for your child to be diagnosed, as MTSS or RTI should *never* delay an evaluation.

The evaluation and diagnosis are just the beginning of the process for receiving services in public schools. Once your child is diagnosed, a meeting will be held with your child's teacher and various other members of the school team. You are allowed to attend this meeting and absolutely should. (Each state is different, so make sure to check the resources section on page 231 to find out how to identify the laws in your state.) At that meeting, the team will determine if your child is eligible for special education services. This is when you get to advocate for what your child needs (see more in chapter 6). Be warned that these meetings can be stressful, so stay positive and calm, have your documentation ready, and know your child's rights.

Every state and school district is slightly different, but here are some of the titles of educators and administrators you'll want to take your questions to:

- Special education teacher
- Reading specialist
- School psychologist
- Speech-language pathologist
- Intervention specialist
- 504 coordinator
- IEP case manager
- Dyslexia coordinator
- MTSS or RTI coordinator
- School administrator

If your child is eligible for special education services and your state provides them, then the supports and services your child will receive are outlined in an individualized education program (IEP), which is a legally binding program once you have signed consent. Remember, you do not have to sign at the end of the meeting. You have the right to take the paperwork with you, think about it at home, and then decide if you consent or not. Once you do, the school must provide what's written in the plan, so make sure it specifies the type and hours of intervention services. Broad goals are not services. You also want to make sure to advocate for your child to be in tier III instruction, which is more intensive than tier II. Remember to keep copies or archives of all documentation and to put all communication in writing.

The figure on page 74 illustrates an overview of the IEP process. While there are some state-specific variations, most of the timelines are based on IDEA. For example, once a parent has acknowledged consent for their child to be diagnosed, the school has 60 calendar days (excluding school breaks of five-plus days) to complete the evaluation and hold an IEP meeting.

If your child is attending a private or independent school, many of these laws don't apply the same way they do in public schools. The school must be ADA-compliant, but it is up to you to share the evaluation with your child's school. Legally, they can't ask if your child has a disability. Each private school is different, but many provide accommodations and some may offer learning support. If your child's private school is unable to offer dyslexia services, your local public school district may be able to provide them, but often in a more limited capacity than if your child was enrolled in the public school.

Overview of the IEP Process

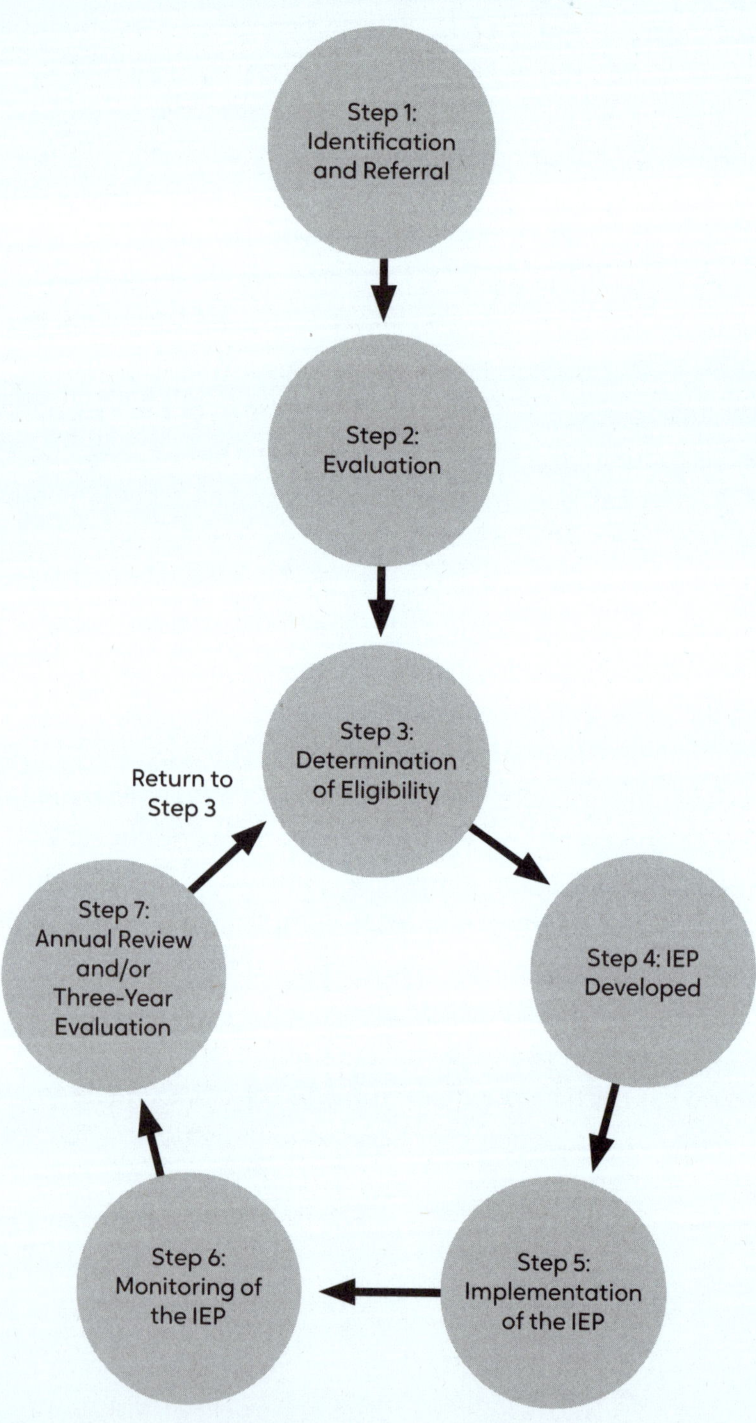

Keeping It All Going

The hard part of receiving a diagnosis and starting intervention can be keeping it all going, especially if insurance doesn't cover the costs. Private therapy and dyslexia intervention can be expensive. With a diagnosis and a letter of necessity from your child's psychologist or assessor, some sessions from a licensed professional may be eligible to be paid for with your health savings account (HSA) or flexible spending account (FSA). These tax-advantaged accounts can help offset costs.

Reach out to local nonprofits or the organizations in the resources section on page 231 as well. These groups may have family support services that can answer your questions, provide recommendations for interventionists, or have documents to help you navigate your local public school system.

They may also suggest local organizations that offer financial assistance or low-cost intervention options and may connect you with scholarships and grants or university programs that provide summer support. Another option is to look for dyslexia summer camps to boost intervention hours.

Specialized Schools

Specialized schools are private or independent schools that offer instruction specifically for someone with dyslexia, oftentimes as their classroom instruction. They generally have high tuition costs, so they aren't an option for everyone. That said, they may offer financial assistance, so it's always worth contacting any in your area. There are many wonderful schools that provide personalized, effective instruction and intervention. If you are considering a specialized or independent school for your child with dyslexia, here are a few things to consider:

Curriculum and Instruction

- What programs are they using to teach reading and writing?
- Do they provide small-group remediation and one-on-one intervention, or is this something your child must get outside of school?
- What assessments do they require to consider a child for admission?

Staffing

- What specialized training do the teachers have?
- What is the student-teacher ratio? (Note: Small class sizes do not necessarily equal a quality education, especially for a child with dyslexia, who will need specialized instruction.)
- Are there specialists on campus, such as speech language pathologists?

School Culture

- How diverse is the student population and staff?
- Is there a religious element to the school?
- How does the school view behavior and discipline?
- What is parent involvement like?

Social/Emotional Support

- Will your child be happy there?
- Is the student population the right size for your child to feel comfortable?
- Are there counselors or other professionals on staff to support academic anxiety?

The Logistics

- How much is tuition? Are there any hidden fees to the academic year, such as field trips?
- Where is the school located?
- Will you be able to easily get your child to school every day?

The Future

- Is the school through-train, meaning does it continue through middle school and/or high school, or will your child have to attend a different school later?
- What opportunities do students typically have postgraduation?

PART II

Strategies

4

Literacy and Language

Part I provided a launching point for you to dive into the at-home strategies to support your child's learning journey that you'll explore here in part II. This chapter focuses on literacy (reading and writing) and language (listening and speaking). While much of what your child needs to learn to read should be provided by their intervention program, you can support their progress at home by practicing the skills they're acquiring in sessions. Some of the strategies in this chapter might seem like schoolwork, but the more correct help your child receives, the faster their development will be. Of course, you'll want to offer your child a reprieve, so find a balance between downtime and practice so that your child stays in tune, happy, and ready to learn.

Common Challenge Areas

So far we've established that dyslexia is a specific learning disability that affects your child's ability to read words, and that phonological processing is often the core deficit. You also know that dyslexia is language-based, so all four language domains (listening, speaking, reading, and writing) are often impacted. Therefore, not only will learning to read likely be hard for your child, but other areas of literacy and language may also be challenging.

While everyone with dyslexia is different, this chapter offers explanations and strategies for 10 aspects of literacy and language development that will likely be impacted by dyslexia. Let's revisit Emma from chapter 2 to better understand how dyslexia can affect each of these areas.

Listening and Speaking

Emma loves chatting with her friends, but she finds it frustrating when she sometimes can't think of the right word even though she knows what she wants to say. She likes to play games like Jenga but finds some word-based games like charades tricky. Sometimes her brain just can't quickly recall the word she wants to call out. She also finds it hard to listen to her teacher occasionally, especially when Mrs. Lopez is giving a lot of instructions or uses too many words to describe what she wants. It's frustrating for Emma when she interprets the teacher incorrectly, at least when words are similar, like "sum" and "some" or "add" and "odd."

Reading

Learning to read requires the mastering of many skills woven together. Some of the underlying processes of reading, like phonemic awareness, are challenging for people with dyslexia because they have trouble interpreting the sounds each letter or group of letters makes. When the brain has a hard time distinguishing between similar sounds and blending sounds together, then reading, which is an extension of those skills, is more difficult.

When foundational skills are weak, reading becomes tricky. This means that when Emma reads, it's slow and choppy because she has poor reading fluency. She makes a lot of mistakes when reading, and because decoding, or breaking apart and sounding out, each word takes so much effort, she's not reading at the right rate or with the correct phrasing. When she reads, she sometimes sounds robotic.

Because Emma uses so much brain power to decode, she doesn't have much left to understand what she reads. In other words, she has poor reading comprehension. For Emma to understand a text, she needs to read with at least 95 percent accuracy. She can achieve this when she reads with Mr. Smith, her dyslexia interventionist, because what he gives her to read includes familiar letter/sound correspondences, word parts, and irregular words she has learned.

There aren't any words in her stories from Mr. Smith that she doesn't know how to break apart and read by herself. For example, she won't be asked to read the word "astronaut" until she's been taught how to find the element "astro" in the word. Sometimes, what Emma is asked to read in class has spelling patterns she hasn't been taught yet. That makes it even harder to read accurately and even harder to understand what she reads.

Vocabulary

Vocabulary is not a language domain, but it does rely on the development of all four language domains (as we covered on page 29). We are exposed to new words through listening and reading, and we need to utilize them through speaking or writing to remember them. The words we are exposed to through reading are different from the ones we hear because the way we write is different from how we speak. Reading, generally, exposes us to more advanced words.

Because reading is hard, Emma understandably avoids it, but this means her ability to expand her vocabulary is limited and negatively affected. She is learning vocabulary words in school, but she is not learning as many new words as her classmates who regularly read. Fortunately, Emma's dad reads to her every evening, which helps close this gap. When we listen to books, we can acquire words we usually wouldn't come across in our daily conversations, which are generally more casual.

Writing

Just like reading, written expression is the culmination of many skills woven together. Writing development is also dependent on reading development. It's difficult to build one without the other. Emma is making progress with Mr. Smith, but she still finds reading difficult, which impacts her writing development. This means her spelling, how she puts sentences together, and the kinds of stories she is currently writing may still not be as strong as those written by her classmates.

We know that Emma's dyslexia makes it hard for her to accurately read a word. We can think of reading (decoding) and spelling (encoding) as two sides of the same coin. If you can read a word, it makes it easier to learn to spell it. On the opposite side, if you have a hard time reading a word, it'll probably make it trickier to learn to spell it. So, because Emma struggles with decoding, she'll also have a hard time encoding.

Emma struggles with phonological awareness skills, which means she has a hard time segmenting the sounds and word parts. Look back at the diagram on page 18 (the one that breaks apart "cat" into sounds and letters). Spelling is the opposite of that. Emma's knowledge of letter/sound correspondences is still developing, so even if she can break apart the sounds, she may not know how to record that sound with a letter or group of letters, which impacts her ability to express herself with the written word.

Emma's spelling is also slower to develop because she reads inaccurately, which makes it harder for the brain to permanently map a word. When a word is mapped onto the brain, we don't have to sound it out anymore, which is known as orthographic mapping. Not only does this support fluent reading, but it also helps us quickly spell words based on the words and patterns we've already mapped.

CHALLENGE 1

Listening Skills

Listening is generally the first language domain we develop. Whether you're an infant or an adult learning a new language, you can understand what you hear before you're able to speak. Listening skills are the foundation for each of the other domains. The main area that is impacted by dyslexia is usually the ability to recognize and manipulate sounds in language, or phonological processing. Some examples include identifying the difference between the phonemes, or sounds, /m/ and /n/; rhyming; and blending sounds together. These skills are required for reading as well as listening, speaking, and writing.

For a child with dyslexia, their listening skills may not be as well developed as their peers'. Following multistep instructions, distinguishing between words that sound similar, following quick conversations, and playing rhyming games may be hard for them. Listening skills can be further impacted for a child with dyslexia who also has coexisting challenges such as auditory processing, slow processing speed, working memory deficits, or executive functioning challenges.

All these skills develop over time, and there are ranges of what is typical for each age and stage. For example, a child in early elementary school may only be able to remember up to three instructions at a time and may take a moment to process speech that includes new words or more complex sentence structures. They may occasionally struggle to remember the right word, especially if it is a new vocabulary word. This is typical, but for someone with dyslexia, their skills may fall outside the range of what's expected for that age and stage.

Every student from ages six to nine should receive instruction in listening comprehension, particularly through regular read-alouds and other activities such as debates and presentations. Your child with dyslexia may need more support in developing listening skills at the same rate as their peers without a learning difference. This is why you can help at home.

Helps with

- Following verbal multistep instructions

What You'll Need

- Nothing

When/Where

- Transitions and new routines at home

Following multistep verbal instructions is one of the most common listening skills challenges for a child with dyslexia. We may not realize it, but so much of a child's day is spent listening to instructions given by an adult and being expected to remember and execute them.

Developmentally, kids ages six to nine generally have a hard time remembering many steps at one time. For any child, including your child with dyslexia, a good rule of thumb is to give only three directions/steps at a time. With a consistent routine, that number can be bumped up to four. These strategies can be used for both one-off instructions and daily routines (see chapter 6 for more information about daily routines).

The key element to all these approaches is to remove the burden of listening comprehension and focus on what's important. These approaches can also be shared with and used by your child's classroom teacher to help your child stay on track with verbal instructions.

Chunking and Repeating

Chunking instructions create bite-sized bits of information that are easier to remember. Here are some helpful tips:

- Focus on removing excess words and say only what is needed.
- Use your fingers to provide a visual reminder of how many steps they need to complete.
- Provide one instruction at a time as you hold up a corresponding finger.

For example, hold up one finger and say, "Get your swimsuit." Hold up a second finger and say, "Get your goggles." Hold up a third finger and say, "Wait by the door." You can then repeat the steps as you hold up your fingers again: "Swimsuit, goggles, wait by the door."

Chunking and Repeating Instructions

"Get your swimsuit."

"Get your goggles."

"Wait by the door."

Wait Time

Giving your child adequate processing time is essential. Some learners with dyslexia, especially those with a coexisting condition, may need up to 20 to 30 seconds to process verbal input before acting on it. This delay may increase depending on the complexity of the task. This means that your child likely just needs more time to hear what you said, think about it, decide what to do with that information, and then act or respond. They may need even more time if what you're asking them to do is complex or novel.

Keep this in mind when you're sharing directions or instructions with your child. Build in wait time to let them process, and then, if necessary, check in with them before repeating your instructions. Here's a sample script to try:

> "(*Your child's name*), connect with me."
>
> *Wait for your child to stop what they're doing and listen.*
>
> "I need you to do three things right now. Put your books away, put your shoes on, meet me at the door."
>
> *Wait for your child to process.*
>
> "Give me a thumbs-up if you know the three things to do right now."
>
> *If you need to, you can repeat the instructions:* "Put your books away, put your shoes on, meet me at the door."

Nonverbal Communication

When someone doesn't understand what we're saying, a common response is to use more words to explain what we mean. For someone with a language-based disorder or other processing issues, this is the opposite of what we want to do. The more we talk, the harder it is for them to understand.

Brainstorm with your child to come up with hand signals you can use as a family to communicate. Let your child take the lead and have fun creating a secret code just for you. Here are some examples:

"Hang tight and stay there."

"We're leaving in five minutes."

Tip: Be mindful of times when your child may not be ready to listen, such as right after school; when they're tired, hungry, or upset; or in loud rooms. In these situations, help your child cope.

CHALLENGE 2

Speaking Skills

The development of speaking skills follows the growth of listening skills and can also be impacted by a diagnosis of dyslexia. Because dyslexia is a language-based learning disorder, we can see ripple effects across all four language domains, not just reading. Dyslexia is not a speech disorder, but it can affect how a person processes and produces language.

For example, a child with dyslexia might struggle to break down or blend sounds when speaking, making it harder for them to correctly pronounce words, especially complex or unfamiliar ones. They may also have trouble distinguishing between similar-sounding words like "ship" and "sheep" or "bat" and "pat." This can lead to mispronunciations, making it harder for others to understand them. A child with dyslexia may also have persistent difficulty producing certain phonemes, or sounds.

Between ages six and nine, most children's speaking skills are growing quickly as they develop more mature and clear language. They are starting to incorporate more complex grammar, a wider vocabulary, and a broader range of conversational skills. They are mastering figurative language and idioms and often have a vocabulary of 3,000 to 6,000 words. A child with dyslexia develops all these same skills but may need help in some areas.

Helps with

- Speaking correctly and clearly
- Addressing grammatical mistakes or mispronunciations

What You'll Need

- Nothing

When/Where

- Conversations with your child

Consistent guidance can support your child's development of speaking skills, particularly if you have noticed the occasional error. As with many factors in your child's development, the key aspect to observe is their rate of progress. If your child is improving with the support they're receiving, you're likely on the right track.

If your child is portraying persistent difficulties with speaking or articulation, consider working with a qualified speech language pathologist. Professional guidance and support could be the missing key to unlocking your child's speaking skills. Your child's school may have already noticed this and talked with you about services, but if they haven't, speak to your child's teacher about your concerns and next steps.

Whether or not your child needs additional support in this area, there are strategies you can use whenever you're interacting with your child. These will encourage your child to incorporate new sentence structures and speech patterns into their language. The biggest thing you can do to help your child is to simply talk with them.

Modeling

You are the expert speaker. Model back-and-forth conversation and incorporate more complex sentence structures when speaking with your child. Show your child what it sounds like to speak in complete sentences. Don't overthink this; simply enjoy having conversations with your child about a range of topics. Use activities, outings, or their own interests to spark conversation. Find moments to chat with your child:

- When you're driving to a birthday party, talk about what they're excited about.
- When you're walking to school, ask them to describe what they ate for breakfast.
- When you're hanging out at home on a weekend morning, talk about their favorite moments from the week before.

Mirroring

Mirroring is a technique you can use to gently encourage your child to correct any mispronunciations or grammatical errors without directly calling out their mistake. When you hear your child speak incorrectly, you can repeat what they said in the correct way.

For example, if your child says, "I runned around the playground." You can respond, "Great! You *ran* around the playground." You can then follow up with an open-ended question, such as "Why were you running on the playground today?"

Remember to remain positive and to not directly correct their mistakes. Instead of saying, "That's wrong," mirror the correct pronunciation or structure. This will help build your child's confidence while reinforcing the speaking skills they are learning.

Using Conjunctions

Use conjunctions like "and," "but," and "when" to extend what your child shares. This is a positive way to encourage them to incorporate more compound and complex sentences into their regular conversations. It's also a great way to help your child share more details about their day. For example, if your child says, "I loved playing at the park," you can add, "until . . ." so they can expand the sentence: "it started to rain." You can use the mnemonic devices "FANBOYS" and "I SAW A WABUB" to help remember the conjunctions.

Coordinating Conjunctions

F	A	N	B	O	Y	S
for	and	nor	but	or	yet	so

Subordinating Conjunctions

I	S	A	W	A	W	A	B	U	B
if	since	as	when	although	while	after	before	until	because

Tip: Be careful not to overcorrect your child, as it may cause frustration and lead to a diminished desire to communicate. Instead, choose one or two errors to focus on during natural conversations.

CHALLENGE 3

Recall and Rapid Naming

Whenever we're talking, our brain is continuously pulling up the right word to use. Sometimes we may not use quite the right word, and other times our brain struggles to find and recall the word in the first place. For someone with dyslexia, processing language and finding the right word can be more difficult. Because of this, your child may at times speak more slowly than their peers, especially when they're trying to organize their thoughts or retrieve a specific word. This can lead to frustration or feelings of self-consciousness.

These challenges are common in the language development of young children, particularly when they are learning new vocabulary words and working through the process of fully understanding and applying them in their everyday language. With dyslexia, these struggles may be extended or prolonged. If your child is managing any speech or language disorders in addition to their dyslexia, you may notice this struggle even more.

Your child may pause during conversations or use general words like "thing" or "that" or more words than necessary to express an idea—for example, "the thing you watch movies on" instead of the "television." Remember to give your child time to process and respond and always be positive when offering help.

Helps with

- Finding or recalling the right word when speaking

What You'll Need

- Nothing

When/Where

- Conversations with your child
- Family game night

Quickly recalling known information, like a list of colors or animals, or thinking of the right word when talking may be tricky for someone with dyslexia, especially if slow processing speed or a language disorder is also present. As your child progresses through their intervention program you should see continued improvement. In addition to the following strategies, make sure your child knows they have a safe space to speak, even if it might take them longer than expected to share their thoughts. Offer space for them and match their pace—when they are comfortable and confident, they can relax, which allows their brain to work stress-free.

Making Mental Connections

When information is organized in your mind, it's easier to retrieve it when you need it. Creating "mental file folders" helps your child make connections between things that fall into larger categories and connect new information to something they already know. Talk with your child about how we can create mental file folders to organize categories in our brain. Some children enjoy making mental file folders of new words they're learning, people they've met, and/or concepts from school. You can try this at the grocery store:

Mental File Folders

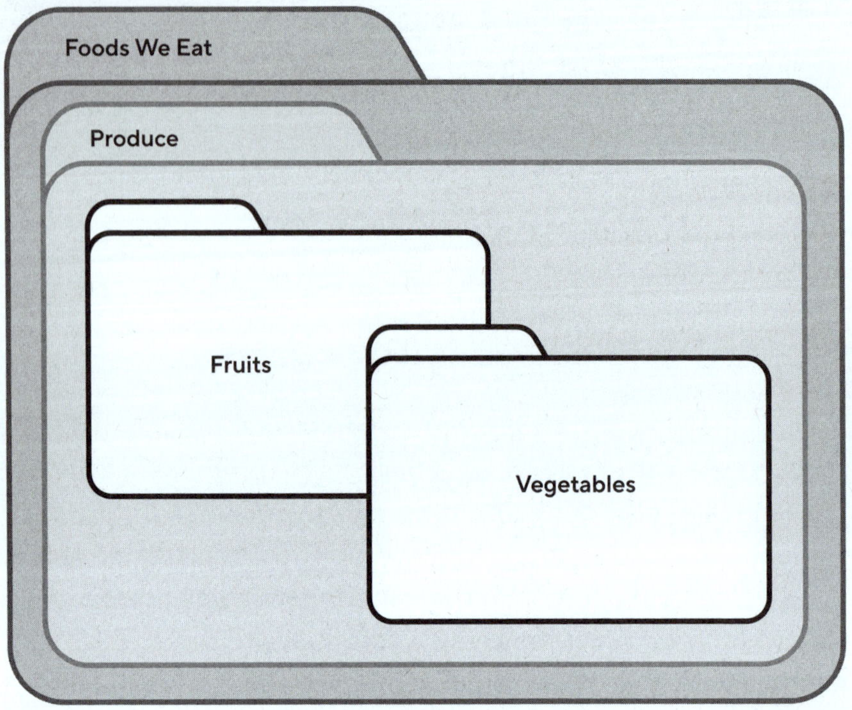

Observe out loud how the store separates food into categories like produce, meats, dairy, beverages, etc. You might say, "These are all different categories of foods we eat. These are all folders within the main folder of foods we eat. Let's walk down the produce aisle and see which fruits and vegetables we can name and put them in our mental file folder under produce."

Cueing

Help cue the word your child is trying to retrieve by describing the object, providing the first sound of the word, or by using visual cues. Here is a sample scenario that might happen at the dinner table:

> Child: "I can't remember what it's called, but I need that thing."
>
> You: "You mean that thing you use to eat soup?"
>
> Child: "Yes!"
>
> You: "It starts with /sp/."
>
> Child: "Spoon!"

Play Language-Based Games

Playing fun language-based games can support your child's ability to describe what they are thinking and to recall known information more quickly, also known as rapid naming. Some games to try are:

- Categories ("Name all the animals you can think of.")
- Animal charades (for example, a hand gesture that mimics a crocodile's snout)
- "I'm thinking of an animal that's . . ."

> **Tip:** While a natural reaction is to jump in and help your child find the right word, this can sometimes lead to increased frustration. Remember to give your child time to process and be successful at their own pace.

CHALLENGE 4

Phonological and Phonemic Awareness

English is a phonemic language, which means it's made up of individual sounds. While the way we record each sound with a letter or group of letters may change depending on various factors in written English, each sound in a word carries meaning. When we change just one sound, we get a different word with an entirely different meaning. For example, "hat" and "hit" are two separate concepts, but there is only one sound that is different. There are a set of skills that allow us to discern and manipulate these differences. They are called phonemic awareness skills and are foundational for learning to read and write. They are part of what allows our brain to fluently read and spell.

Phonological awareness, meanwhile, is the larger category and is our ability to play with the individual sounds or chunks of sounds in our language. The figure on page 99 shows the range of phonological awareness skills and the sequence in which they typically develop. Rhyming is one of the first phonological awareness skills acquired when young children are developing their ability to play with language and therefore is an early indicator of a strong reader. It's typically mastered by around ages four and a half to five.

The strategies in this section are all about helping your child boost their phonological and phonemic awareness skills, which are essential when learning to read. Your child will need extra time to practice them because learning how to rhyme and play with the sounds of language won't come intuitively or quickly for someone with dyslexia. If your child is also having a hard time making the sounds correctly, then they may need even more time to practice. With these strategies, you can encourage your child to build their rhyming skills, as well as their abilities to put together sounds to make a word and break apart a word into individual sounds. You will practice each of these skills separately so that your child can focus on strengthening them one at a time.

Phonological Awareness and Development

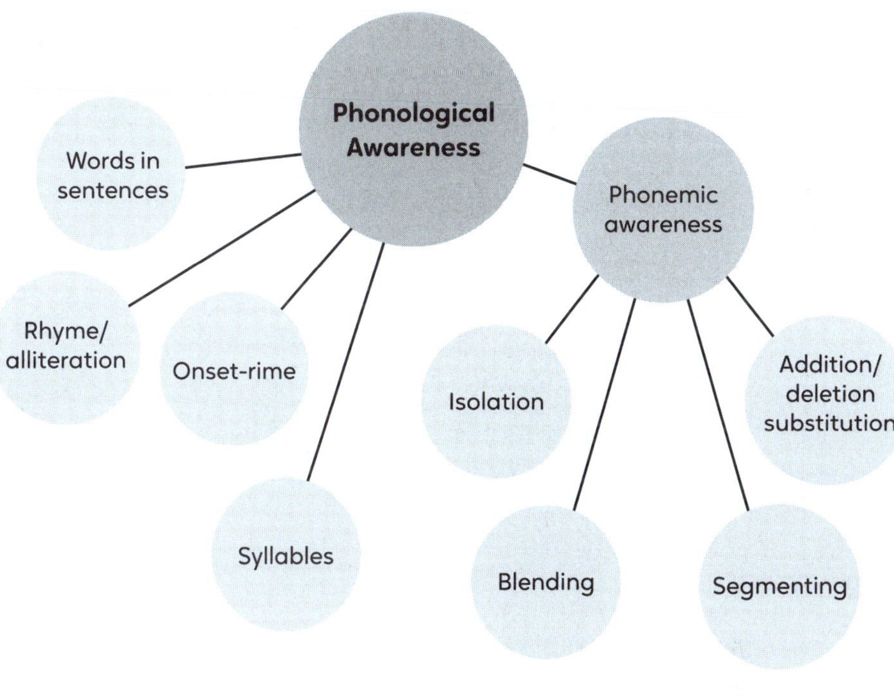

Helps with

- Practicing skills the brain needs to accurately read and write individual words

What You'll Need

- Rhyming storybooks
- Elkonin boxes (a visual tool to help your child see how many sounds are in each word; also called sound boxes)
- Counters, magnets, or your child's favorite cereal

When/Where

- Warm-ups before reading or writing
- Conversations with your child

Rhyming, blending sounds, and segmenting sounds are essential skills to become a fluent reader and writer.

- Rhyming words are words that have the same or similar ending sounds, like "fish" and "dish."
- Blending sounds is when we put sounds together to make a new word.
- Segmenting sounds is when we break apart the sounds in a word.

Help your child build these skills with repeated practice at home using these strategies. Inject as much fun into these activities as you can and connect with your child's teacher and interventionist to know where your child is in their learning journey.

Rhyming

There are many ways to play with rhyming words with your child. Have fun and let your silly side run free. Here are some ideas:

- Read rhyming books.
- Sing rhyming songs and nursery rhymes.
- Take turns thinking of rhyming words.
- Play rhyming games like matching and sorting (or search "rhyming games" online).
- Point out rhymes in everyday conversations.

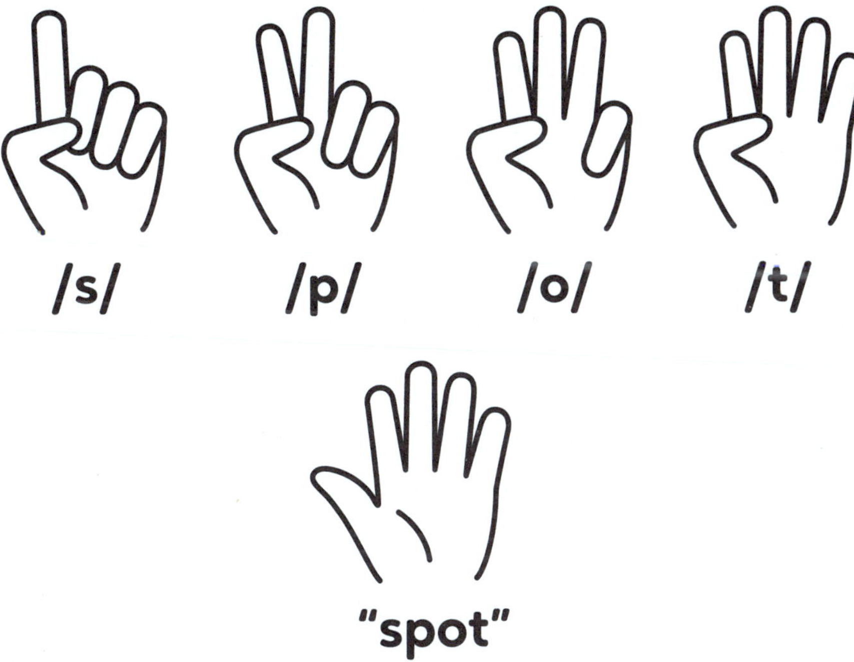

Blending or Putting Sounds Together

Practice blending specific words by saying each sound as you raise a finger (see diagram above). Your child can then say the word as you open your hand. Using your fingers provides a visual cue to your child of how many sounds they should be listening for. If your child needs a more accessible starting point, try blending the onset and the rime, or the first sound and the rest of the word. For example, /h/ and /ăt/ to say "hat."

Segmenting or Breaking Sounds Apart

Use Elkonin boxes and multisensory items such as counters or magnets to break apart words. Elkonin boxes provide a visual reminder for your child of how many sounds they should be listening for. You'll say the word and your child will tap out the sounds or slide counters or magnets into each box. Alternatively, use your child's favorite cereal, which they can eat after breaking apart the word for added fun.

For example, as you can see in the diagram on page 103, the top row has three boxes. That means the word will have three sounds; for example, the word "top" has /t/ /ŏ/ /p/. A word like "splash" has five sounds, /s/ /p/ /l/ /ă/ /sh/, so you'd use the row with five boxes. The diagram also includes an example of the word "brakes" being broken apart into its five sounds. Remember, this isn't about how many *letters* are in the word, but how many *sounds* you hear when you say the word.

Use this script to practice breaking apart the sounds in a word:

> "I'm going to say the word, and you'll tap out how many sounds you hear."
>
> *Your child looks at you and listens.*
>
> "Sit."
>
> *Your child taps out /s/ /ĭ/ /t/ with one sound in each box.*

Tip: When rhyming, encourage your child to use nonsense words if they want. Also, phonological awareness has nothing to do with the letters on the page, so don't worry about how words are spelled, just focus on the sounds you hear. Finally, you may want to work on just one skill or activity at a time. These games may be taxing for your child, so keep practice short and sweet.

Elkonin Boxes

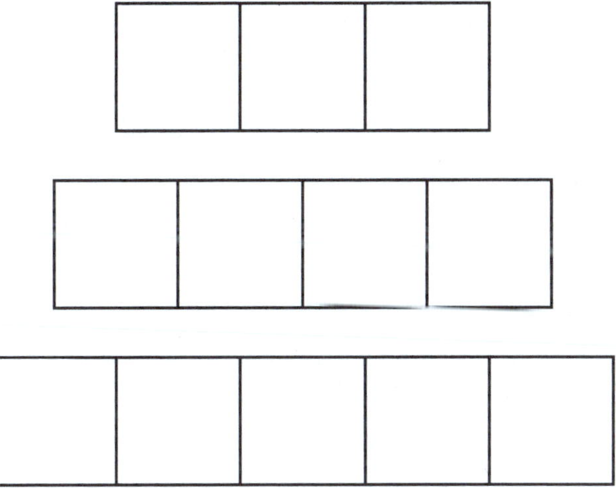

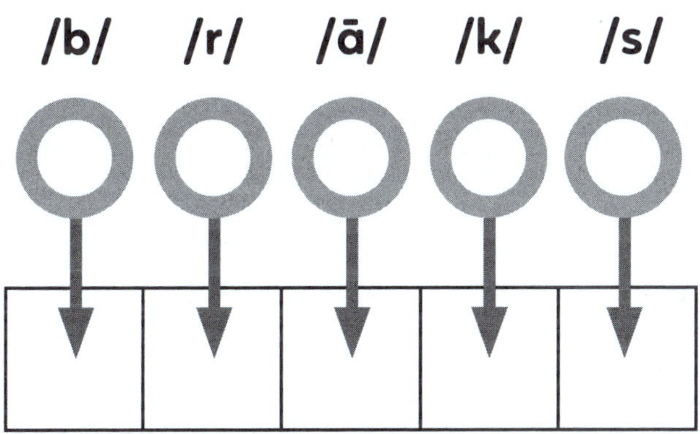

CHALLENGE 5

Decoding and Word Recognition Skills

Decoding and word recognition, or the ability to break apart, sound out, and put words back together to read them, will likely be a pervasive challenge for your child. Supporting your child's decoding at home is key, especially during the initial stages of their intervention program.

Being a skilled reader means you can accurately read the words on the page and understand them. When we're able to do this, we comprehend what we read. The Simple View of Reading, a formula introduced by Philip B. Gough and William E. Tunmer in 1986, can help us visualize this process.

The Simple View of Reading

Based on Gough and Tunmer (1986, 1990)

Helps with

- Accurately breaking apart and reading words

What You'll Need

- Plastic letters, magnetic letters, and grapheme cards (Use letters you already have at home or purchase magnetic ones online; I recommend using sets with only two colors: one for consonants and one for vowels. See the resources section on page 232 for a link to free grapheme cards from the University of Florida Literacy Institute.)

When/Where

- Practice time at home

Accurate word recognition of regular words is all about decoding, or breaking apart words into letters and chunks to sound out or read each part, and then putting them together to read the word. We learn to do this by looking at individual letters, groups of letters, and parts.

With a word like "chatting," we can see the individual letter/sound correspondences, but we can also see the suffix at the end of the word. We can break apart and sound out "chat," and "ing" can be recognized as a part we already know how to read. For example:

chat + ing → chatting

chatt ing

ch = /ch/ a = /ă/ t = /t/

Learning how to break apart words is a big part of an effective dyslexia intervention program. How words are formed may not be readily apparent to your child, and these strategies can help. With practice, your child will learn to recognize chunks and see the patterns in words, which will help build their ability to perform the task quickly and efficiently. At first, it may seem like your child is just memorizing chunks and patterns, but their eventual understanding of how words and spelling patterns work will lead to your child independently and automatically recognizing the patterns and applying them without even thinking about it. You can also be a good model for your child by sounding out a new word when reading together to show them that the reading skills they're learning can help even outside of schoolwork.

Chaining

Use magnetic letters, and later grapheme cards, to practice quickly reading similar words. Start with a word your child knows the letter/sound correspondences of. Read that word and then change one letter at a time to read a new word. This is called chaining because you're linking similar words together by only changing one letter or sound at a time. When they're ready, make the words longer and include suffixes like "-less" or "-ful." Encourage your child to recognize which parts didn't change and to hold on to them as they read the new word.

Here's an example of how you can change one sound to make new words:

1. Spell "hat" with the magnetic letters.
2. Ask, "What does this say?"
3. Change the "a" to "i" to spell "hit."

4. Ask, "What does it say now?"

5. Change the "t" to "p."

6. Ask, "What does it say now?"

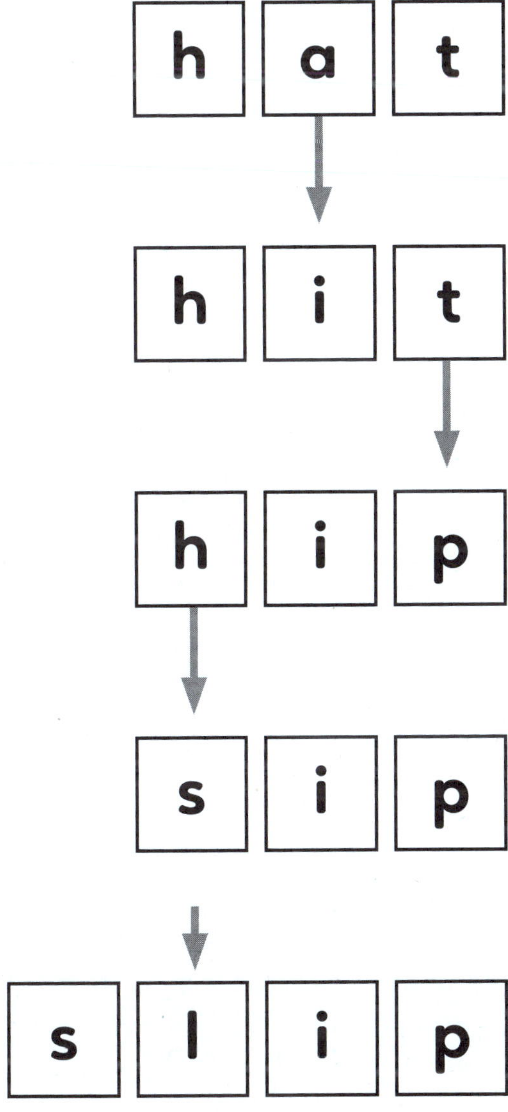

Practice Word Parts

Use flash cards, chants, letter tiles, and fun pens to practice reading and spelling word parts, such as suffixes. The great thing about suffixes is that you cannot change how they are spelled. Once your child knows that suffix, they will always know how to read that chunk in any word they come across. Common suffixes for early readers include:

- -ing
- -ed
- -s
- -ful
- -less
- -er
- -ly

Here's an example of how to create a chant with the suffix "ed":

1. Name the letters: "e-d"
2. Say a keyword (or more if there are multiple ways to read that suffix):
    - "folded /ĭd/"
    - "sailed /d/"
    - "jumped /t/"
3. Give the meaning of the suffix: "happened in the past"

Decodable Books

Connected decodable books are meant to support decoding skills but also paired with a specific point in your child's learning-to-read journey and include only concepts they have been explicitly taught. Through contextual practice, connected decodable books can help reinforce the letter/sound correspondences, word parts, and decoding strategies your child has learned.

Decodable books are books that include regular words that are read the way we expect them to and common irregular words that have likely been taught to your child. (For example, a word like "cow" reads the way we expect because the letter "c" makes the /k/ sound and the vowel pair "ow" makes the /ou/ sound. A word like "island" is irregular because the letter "s" is unexpectedly silent.)

Check with your child's teacher and interventionist to determine which books are the right fit. Choose carefully, as some books may include words your child can't accurately read yet. These are still great options to read to your child but not for their independent reading—yet. Some small publishers provide great options for decodables. One of my favorites is High Noon Books, listed in the resources section on page 231.

Tip: Your child's reading development is at a fragile point. They are just learning to break the alphabetic code, and it can be easy for their confidence to take a hit. If your child is struggling, always step in to help. It's far better to help them with a word than for them to struggle until they are frustrated.

CHALLENGE 6

Reading Fluency

Reading fluency is the mark of an accurate reader and is the bridge between word recognition and comprehension. When we read accurately, at an appropriate rate, and with good expression, we are reading fluently. This basically means that it sounds like we're talking when we're reading. When we read fluently, we're far more likely to understand what we are reading.

Here are the three components of reading fluency with examples:

Accuracy

- Correctly reads words without persistent mistakes.
- 95 percent accuracy is a good goal.

Rate (Speed)

- Reads at an appropriate pace, similar to how you would talk.
- Smooth word recognition is the goal.

Expression (Prosody)

- Reads with the natural flow and rhythm similar to how you would talk.
- Uses appropriate expression to reflect punctuation.
- Meaning is the goal.

Reading fluency is crucial as it is the bridge between decoding and comprehending. To build reading fluency, your child needs to build some prerequisite skills. Like a ladder, you can't reach the top without climbing your way up. As the progression below illustrates, if your child reaches the fluency rung of the ladder, then they're ready to learn new vocabulary

The National Reading Panel's Five Pillars of Reading

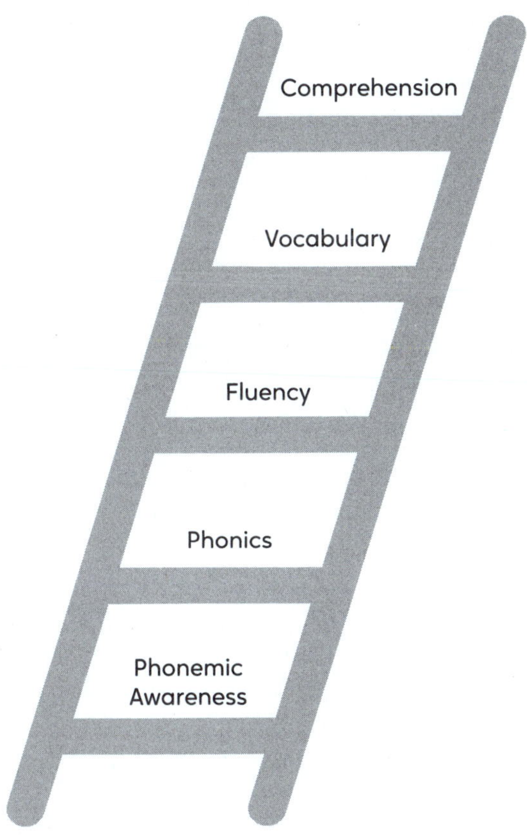

words and ultimately understand what they're reading, which is comprehension.

For your child, reading fluency will likely be a challenge. They may be spending so much time and effort decoding words that it impacts their reading accuracy and slows down their rate. They may be so focused on decoding that they don't even notice punctuation or attend to meaning and, therefore, read without expression, also known as the disfluent phase. Every child learning to read will experience it, but your child with dyslexia will need more time to practice to move toward being a more fluent reader.

Helps with

- Reading fluently

What You'll Need

- Books, passages, and words from your child's intervention program

When/Where

- Reading at home

Automaticity is the key to fluency. This means your child doesn't have to sound out a word but can read it on sight. Automaticity comes from repeated practice. Many people think practice makes perfect, but really, practice makes permanent. If we do something incorrectly when we practice, we're learning to do it the wrong way, so make practice accurate.

When a child reads a word correctly several times, that word becomes orthographically mapped, or stamped into the brain. Help your child accurately read a word multiple times until they can read it on sight, or without having to sound it out. A child with dyslexia may need to read a word 10 times or more to have it mapped into their brain. This number may go down as intervention proceeds and as they grow and develop along their academic journey. These strategies help you build in practice so that your child's fluency will improve.

Repeated Readings

When possible, dedicate a special time in your child's day to reading the words and stories their interventionist sends home. You can make this part of their homework routine or have a special time right after their afternoon snack. If possible, try to avoid doing it right before bedtime as reading then could be more difficult. Keep bedtime separate and make it a meaningful time to simply enjoy sharing stories with your child, which can include books you read to them, stories you make up together from the pictures in a book, or listening to audiobooks while following along with a physical copy of the book.

Reader's Theater

Help your child bring their books to life by turning them into plays. Having fun with reader's theater is a great way to incorporate repeated readings into your child's practice without having it feel repetitive. The more they can accurately read the words, the stronger their fluency will become.

After your child has read a story, have them choose either the whole story or a passage to act out. Don't worry about elaborate props; just have fun. The purpose is to let your child's creativity run free. You can involve other members of your family as characters, or your child can act out multiple parts by swapping one piece of costume for another. Your child can use their favorite stuffed animals as the audience and design posters to announce their upcoming production.

Tip: Remember to make repeated readings fun. If your child is reluctant to practice, incorporate a sticker or tally chart to record how many times they've read the book.

CHALLENGE 7

Reading Comprehension

Reading comprehension is the culmination of many interwoven skills and requires us to accurately read words on the page and have strong language comprehension skills. Reading comprehension is when those skills are active together—the ultimate goal of reading.

On page 104, we looked at the Simple View of Reading formula. In the early 1990s, Dr. Hollis Scarborough expanded on this model, demonstrating how the different strands of reading are all interconnected, yet independent of one another. Dr. Scarborough's Reading Rope model further demonstrates the strands of reading and was first published in the *Handbook of Early Literacy Research* in 2001. You can see the various strands required for reading comprehension and how language comprehension is just as important as word recognition on page 115.

For all kids, listening comprehension skills remain stronger than reading comprehension skills well into middle school and even the beginning of high school. A child with dyslexia may never have reading comprehension skills that are as strong as their listening comprehension skills, but practicing reading comprehension strategies while listening to stories will bolster their reading comprehension development.

Scarborough's Reading Rope

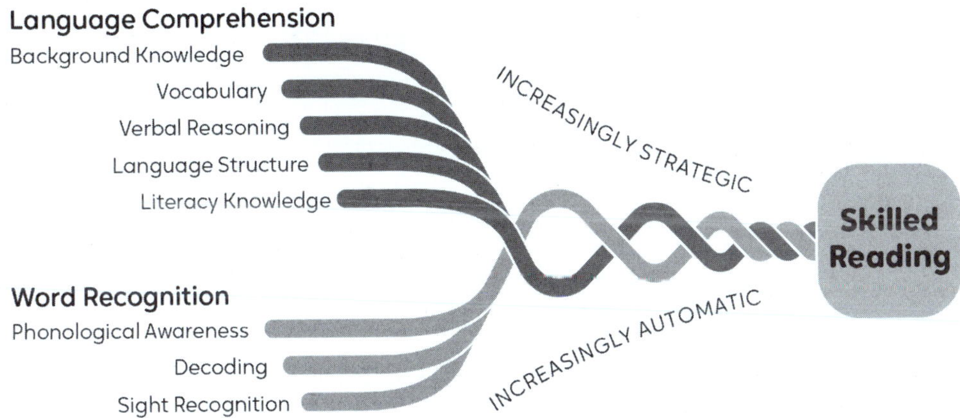

Helps with

- Reading comprehension skills

What You'll Need

- Your child's favorite books

When/Where

- Sharing books at home

The more you read to your child, the stronger your bond will be, the more words they will learn, the more likely they will be to love literature, and the stronger their social/emotional skills will become. To employ these strategies, find time in your day to share books with your child, like at bedtime or with audiobooks in the car.

When choosing books to share, remember that you'll be reading them to your child; these are not books your child can read by themselves. Look for books with characters, locations, or topics that interest your child, whether that's fiction, nonfiction, or chapter books. Talk with your child to see if there is a longer book they have been wanting to read. As long as your child is interested, there is no wrong book or time to read together.

Making Predictions

Practice making predictions as you read to your child. This means they are making an educated guess about what will happen next in the story. This is a key good-reader skill that builds critical-thinking abilities and helps your child engage more deeply with the story. Here are some prediction prompts:

Plot

- What do you think this story is about?
- What do you think will happen next?
- What clues from what we've read so far make you think this?
- What kind of ending do you expect will happen?

Characters

- How do you think the characters will react?
- How do you think the characters will change as the story continues?

Setting

- How might the setting impact what comes next?
- Could the setting change in a way that affects the plot or characters?

Summarizing

Summarizing a story or nonfiction text your child has heard is a great way for them to demonstrate what they remember or learned from the book. Help your child practice retelling the story as they listen, and when the book is finished, use one of the following summarizing strategies:

Fiction Books and Stories

- "Somebody wanted . . . but . . . so then . . ." For example, "The Big Bad Wolf wanted to eat Little Red Riding Hood, but the Huntsman arrived at the house and attacked the Big Bad Wolf, so then Little Red Riding Hood was saved."
- Use the Five "Wh" Questions:
  - Who: character
  - When and where: setting
  - What and why: plot

Nonfiction Books and Articles

- The main idea (e.g., Elephants live in social groups.)
- The cause and effect (e.g., Gravity causes things to fall.)
- The sequence (e.g., 10 steps to build a toy car)
- The problem and solution (e.g., If it rains, use an umbrella.)

Inferencing

Inferencing is an important life skill and is necessary to think critically about what we're reading. It's a simple equation to create an inference:

an inference = what you see/hear/read + what you know

Help your child practice inferencing skills as you share books together, and use these questions and prompts to guide their thinking:

What You Heard

- What just happened in the story?
- What did we just learn about the main idea?

What You Know

- What do you know about characters or setting like this?
- What do you already know about this topic?

What You Infer

- What can you infer the character is thinking or feeling?
- What can you infer about this topic?

Tip: Don't worry about practicing all these skills every time you read. Sometimes, just enjoy the moment.

CHALLENGE 8

Vocabulary Acquisition

Vocabulary is an essential piece of being a skilled reader. The more words we know, the better we understand what we are reading. As the books we read increase in complexity, there are more and more words we need to understand. The older we get as readers, the greater the expectations on our vocabulary are.

Acquiring new vocabulary is partially a natural process and partly due to exposure and explicit practice. How your child learns new words will change as they age. Prior to being a fluent reader, they will primarily learn new words through conversations or stories they hear. After becoming a fluent reader, this shifts to learning new words from books they read independently. This is an important transition because the vocabulary we use in everyday speech and in books can be quite different in terms of complexity, formality, and richness.

The number of words your child is exposed to is important as well. Students in kindergarten through third grade are typically introduced to up to 2,000 new words a year. Their vocabulary could be growing by 300 to 400 new words each school year.

Regardless of how young children are exposed to new words, when we learn new vocabulary in context and with connections, that's when they best stick. Try these strategies to help your child retain and apply new words.

Helps with

- Learning new words

What You'll Need

- Your child's favorite read-aloud books
- Note cards and construction paper

When/Where

- Reading and conversations with your child

Your child may not be willing to spend much time reading independently, which limits their exposure to the vocabulary typically used in written language and slows their vocabulary development. This may make reading comprehension even harder, which might further impact their willingness to read new books. This downward spiral that can affect children with dyslexia is called the Matthew effect. Of course, technology is impacting the reading trends of all ages, but for your child with dyslexia, it is crucial to expose them to new vocabulary on a regular basis.

Recognizing New Words and Making Connections

During a natural part of your conversation, help your child recognize new words. First, gauge your child's emotional bandwidth for learning something new so that it never feels like a big task to think about the new words they're learning. You can also check in with your child to see what new words they want to learn, perhaps to describe a new sport or hobby. Here are a few questions you can use to start the conversation; choose just one or two at a time:

- What new word did you just hear?
- What do you think that means?
- What other word did that make you think of?
- Do you know a word that means something similar?

Building Background Knowledge

Help your child build background knowledge about the world around them. The more we know about history, cultures, science, and everyday concepts, the better we can connect new words to what we already know.

Put a map up in the family room and look at it whenever you and your child watch a new movie that takes place in another state or country or when you try different cuisines. Make it a game with your child to find that location on the map and talk about what you learned or how people in that part of the world might live.

Shades of Meaning

Practice identifying the shades of meanings between groups of words with similar definitions. We have a rich language full of synonyms that aren't exactly the same. The better we understand these groups of words, the stronger the connections will be between words we have learned.

Here are a few fun examples of how to explore shades of meaning:

- Find room to act out the different ways to move on two feet, such as walk, strut, saunter, slide, hop, stroll, march, and pace.

- Dump out your child's box of crayons and explore similar colors.
- Use an emotions chart, which you can easily find online, to investigate feelings with similar but slightly different meanings, like angry and enraged.

Tip: Learning new vocabulary doesn't need to be a chore. Embrace small moments with your child to incorporate new words into conversations or research new words together you want to add to your family's lexicon.

CHALLENGE 9

Encoding Skills

As you know, when we spell (or encode), we break down the sounds we hear and write them down. To decode, we break apart what we see to read it. There is much overlap between the skills required to encode and decode. This is why it makes sense that your child may have a hard time learning to spell words correctly when they have difficulty reading.

Breaking apart the word we hear to spell is more than just listening to the sounds. Spelling is the overlap of the sounds, the word parts, the meaning, and the origin of the word. For young children learning how to spell, you often hear teachers encouraging them to sound out a word. This is an important strategy, but the structure and meaning of the word are just as important as the sounds. This approach is even more important for your child with dyslexia.

The figure below examines why it's important to think about more than just what you hear when spelling. While everyone's pronunciation may be slightly different, this is an example of two words that sound similar but have different structures and meanings.

Helps with

- Accurately spelling words

What You'll Need

- Elkonin boxes (see page 103)
- Note cards
- The same plastic letters, magnetic letters, and grapheme cards from Literacy and Language Challenge 5

When/Where

- Spelling practice at home

English has regular and irregular words. This means we have words that are spelled the way we expect them to, like "hat," and words that have one or more sounds that are spelled differently than we expect, like "said." Up to 87 percent of spellings in the English language are predictable. This means that as your child progresses through their intervention program, the way words are spelled will start to make more sense. This is good news!

Let's take a look at a few different strategies that you can use at home to support your child as they learn to break apart regular words and memorize the spellings of irregular words. These strategies are three of the best ways to help your child practice their spelling skills, as they can be used on almost any word they try to spell. Make sure to connect with your child's teacher and dyslexia interventionist to know where they are in their learning-to-spell journey. This way you can reinforce what they're learning at home.

Breaking Apart Words

You learned how to use Elkonin boxes on page 103. In that strategy, you were using the boxes to help your child blend the sounds in a word. Now use them to break apart the sounds in a word.

First, make sure your child knows how many sounds to listen for. Once they have that in mind, you can help them use the boxes to break apart the sounds and then connect each sound with the right letter or letters.

Here's a script to use with your child:

> "The words we're going to be spelling will have four sounds. This means we're going to use the row with four boxes."
>
> *Your child acknowledges this.*
>
> "I'm going to say the word, then you'll say it, then you'll break it apart."
>
> *Say the word.*
>
> *Ask your child to repeat the word.*
>
> *Help your child tap out each sound they hear.*
>
> *Use magnetic letters, grapheme cards, or a marker to spell each sound they hear.*

See the example that follows using the word "slick." Again, you'll say the word. Your child will repeat the word. They will break apart the sounds they hear and then write the word.

Some words may have consonant blends, such as "strap," in which multiple consonants are strung together. Recognizing each of the consonant sounds may be tricky for some children with dyslexia. If your child is struggling to accurately break apart consonant blends, say, "That was very close, but there is a sound hiding in the word. Listen again as I stretch out the word." Then pronounce the word slowly, making sure to stress each consonant sound.

Sounding Out "Slick" Using Elkonin Boxes

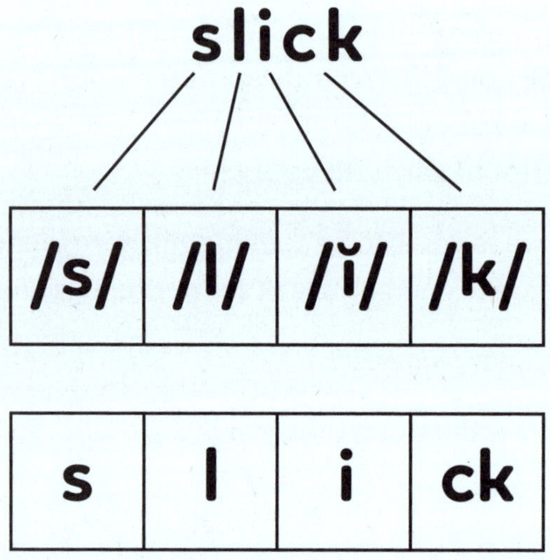

Suffixes

Identifying suffixes is an important step in being a skilled speller. Help your child practice breaking apart base words and suffixes. Here are some examples:

- "Playing" → play + ing
- "Walked" → walk + ed
- "Sleepless" → sleep + less

Here are a few ideas to make this more fun for you and your child:

- Let them choose the words.

- Pretend to be word doctors and cut apart the suffix from the base word.
- Play word detectives and look for suffixes in books and magazines.
- Make word part puzzles and create silly words.

Irregular Words

Use kinesthetic approaches with your child to help them memorize how to spell irregular words. Kinesthetic, or moving, learning is part of the multisensory teaching approach, which has been shown to be important for children with dyslexia. When your child is incorporating other senses into their learning, they're strengthening the connections their brain makes. Check with your child's teacher or dyslexia interventionist for a list of irregular words they've been taught. Some programs may call these heart words, high-frequency words, or sight words.

Here are some multisensory ways to practice spelling irregular words. Your child will:

- Clap their hands as they name each letter in the word and then jump when they say the whole word.
- Name the letter as they write or slide letter tiles into place to spell the word.
- Dribble a ball as they name each letter before tossing the ball to you as they say the word.

Tip: If your child's handwriting development is slower than expected, use magnetic letters or grapheme cards to practice spelling. This can help remove the extra burden of writing the letter while still practicing their spelling.

CHALLENGE 10

Written Expression

Reading and writing development go hand in hand. Reading always comes first. The stronger our reading skills become, the stronger our writing skills become for two reasons: we usually understand language (receptive) before we can use it to communicate (expressive), and written language often uses different words and structures than spoken language.

Just like with reading, written expression is the balance of encoding and language skills. Your child needs to know how to get the words onto the page in a way that someone else can understand and what to say and how to say it. They are learning handwriting, spelling, grammar, and punctuation, while also learning creativity, storytelling, organization, and the author's craft techniques.

For children in the early elementary years, writing can be challenging. They often don't yet have the skills to write down their thoughts, which are becoming increasingly complex as they mature. Their hands may not be strong enough yet to write for extended periods, making writing even harder. Because of this, their expressive capabilities while speaking will far outshine their abilities in writing. This is absolutely normal for all children.

Quality instruction for all young learners includes building writing skills through their speaking skills. Children are encouraged to embrace their inherent imagination as they build foundational skills like learning to speak in complete sentences, write paragraphs, and create organized stories. As they strengthen all these skills, they become increasingly gifted writers.

Helps with

- Building written expression

What You'll Need

- A variety of small natural and synthetic items ("loose parts")
- Paper and crayons/markers
- Fun writing instruments
- A journal of your child's choosing

When/Where

- Creating stories at home

Many children are natural storytellers gifted with endless imaginations. For some children with dyslexia, these gifts can shine even more brightly. They may be exceptional orators or creative thinkers. You can help your child recognize and hone their unique gifts of expression, even if writing and spelling are challenging. This may be even more necessary if your child is experiencing difficulties with handwriting or fine motor skills, or if they also have other learning differences in addition to dyslexia.

Just like with reading and listening comprehension skills, written expression skills can be developed through speaking. Your child can learn how to effectively share their thoughts and stories orally while also developing their writing, handwriting, and spelling skills. Over time and with the right support, your child's technical skills can catch up with their expressive abilities, which will help them excel as capable writers. These strategies will help them on their way.

Telling Stories

Children are natural storytellers and want to share their creative ideas. For a child with dyslexia, though, it can be frustrating to have to write down their stories. It can be so overwhelming that they may not even want to share their stories anymore. So find fun ways to let your child be the storyteller without having to write it out.

You can do this by providing loose parts and household props to let your child's imagination flow without restraint. This can be anything regularly found at home or in craft stores, like sticks, stones, yarn, shells, buttons, bits of fabric, or pieces of cardboard. Encourage your child's imagination, problem-solving, and storytelling skills as they manipulate, combine, and rearrange the parts to create their own unique stories.

You can also get involved in your child's storytelling by being the recorder.

- Use a device to record a video or audio of your child sharing their story after they've created it.
- Offer to write down their words so that they can see their ideas transformed into writing without feeling the pressure of having to do it themselves.

If your child is stuck with the creative process, try these ideas to encourage them along:

- Take turns creating or expanding on a story.
- Re-create a story they already know.
- Ask questions:
    - What adventure will your friend go on today?
    - Where is this story going to happen?

Drawing

Encourage your child's creative storytelling through intentional drawing. Have fun finding arts and crafts supplies they can use to make their ideas come to life. You can check out your local thrift shops for materials as well.

As your child draws, encourage them to add details and multiple pages to illustrate their unique narrative. Detailed illustrations lead to detailed written stories, so help them practice adding descriptive details and multiple creative elements.

Low-Stakes Writing Tasks

Come up with fun and quick writing activities to boost your child's confidence as a writer. Some ideas include:

- A wish list of toys they would like
- A postcard to a friend or family member
- A letter to a favorite stuffed animal
- Labels for their toy bins

If you have time, head to a discount store to buy fun writing tools, journals, and paper. Give your child a budget and let them choose their supplies.

Tip: Technology can be a big support for children with learning differences. Learning to properly touch type can ease the physical burden of handwriting. Consider a typing program for your second or third grader, or when your child's hands are large enough to correctly use a keyboard.

How to Encourage Reading Time

You know how important it is for your child to practice what they are learning, so this is all about gentle encouragement.

- Create an inviting routine around reading time. Perhaps you'll have a small snack and beverage together and then head to the reading area. If your child is reading on their own, read your own book at the same time, if possible. Be available to offer help if needed, and take time to show them you recognize how hard they're working.
- Let your child take ownership of building reading routines. You can talk with your child about where in their afternoon and weekend schedule they would like to build in 10 to 20 minutes to read. Help your child create their own personalized reading corner in an area you would generally read in, too. They can help decorate the space to make it a place they want to spend time in.
- Include a variety of books in the area that are appropriate for your child's current reading level. Check with your child's teacher and dyslexia interventionist for ideas. For some young readers, book series can be a great way to get them hooked on reading. The familiar characters and predictable plots can reduce the cognitive load of comprehension, making the stories new but familiar. You can also find high-interest, low-level readers from specialized publishers (see the resources section on page 231).

If your child is in the middle of an effective intervention program, be aware that they may not have the energy to read at home after a long day at school. If this is the case, read to them instead.

Reflection

Just as it is with your child, it's important to recognize your effort and celebrate your progress. After you have tried the strategies, take time to reflect and tweak your approach if needed. Here are some questions to help guide your reflection:

What progress have I seen?

____

____

____

____

Am I recognizing the effort my child and I are making?

____

____

____

____

____

What has my child learned? What have I learned?

____

____

____

____

Am I being patient and positive with myself and my child?

Have I been using these strategies consistently?

Do I need to make any adjustments to the strategies I've tried?

How is my child feeling about these new approaches? What can they share with me at this point?

5

Social and Emotional Development

Sometimes you may notice your child getting frustrated, struggling with their confidence, or coming home from school looking defeated. Perhaps you've seen them get upset when homework time rolls around or avoid hanging out with peers. This is normal. This chapter helps you prepare for the social and emotional challenges your child may be facing as a learner with dyslexia. While you can't change the world for your child, this chapter guides you in helping them navigate social situations and deal with their big emotions.

Common Challenge Areas

Since young children don't yet have the emotional maturity to process the difficult emotions that tend to arise when they are struggling with reading, it can affect their self-confidence and self-esteem can plummet, which can then impact their social relationships. In a learning environment that is less supportive, these effects can be even more impactful. Guiding your child with dyslexia as they navigate their big emotions can invite conversations and opportunities for your child to cope, regulate big feelings, build trust, and overcome any social hurdles while learning to read.

Typical Social Development

To better understand social and emotional challenges a child with dyslexia might face, let's begin by looking at what typical social development looks like in the table below. Remember, every child is different, so these are just broad trends.

Age 6	• Able to follow simple rules and directions. • Learn adult social skills like giving praise and apologizing for mistakes. • Start to prefer to be with and relate to groups of friends. • Imaginative play becomes more complex.
Ages 7–8	• Can fully understand and follow rules. • Build a deeper understanding of relationships and responsibilities. • Start to develop a sense of morality. • Identify more closely with other children and may find a best friend.
Age 9	• Spending time with friends starts to become even more important. • Become increasingly independent and capable of decision-making. • Still seek positive, nurturing relationships with caregivers to establish self-confidence and self-assurance.

What You Might Observe with Your Child

Physical, mental, or emotional factors can affect our ability to cope with difficulties. For example, a lack of sleep, poor food choices, and feeling unwell can reduce our emotional bandwidth. It might look like taking things more personally or hyper-focusing on what went wrong. This is true for anyone, of any age. In children, however, because their prefrontal cortex isn't fully developed, they usually don't understand that their physical, mental, and/or emotional tank is on or nearing empty. They may not even realize when they're hungry, let alone when they're stressed or anxious.

As adults, part of our role is to help children recognize their needs and teach them how to meet them. Learn to recognize or be sensitive to when your child's reserves start to dwindle due to physical, mental, or emotional factors, and step in as needed to support your child in whatever is expected of them at that time. Acknowledge that what you personally find easy can be challenging and maybe even impossible for them. When we come from a place of understanding, we can have the empathy and patience necessary to help a child who is having a hard time socially or emotionally.

Be aware that your child with dyslexia may face unique social and emotional challenges or may feel the weight of the same challenges more intensely. Their capacity for struggle may be more limited than their peers', especially after a long day at school. Here are some examples:

- You may notice their confidence takes a dip as the reading demands in the classroom increase. Even with the right intervention, it will take time for a child with dyslexia to catch up.

- Typically, around the age of seven, or moving toward second grade, children start to become more self-aware. They may start to realize what they can't do and what their classmates can and may struggle to accept this.
- Your child may freeze when asked to read in class or become overwhelmed by seemingly simple tasks. Talk with your child's teacher to help them understand why it's important to not call on your child to read in front of the class.
- Your child may become automatically triggered by just being in an academic setting. Spend time reflecting on what challenges your child is facing so that you can be better prepared to help them navigate these hurdles. Talk with your child to understand the rhythm of their day and what they find tricky.

Your child may not yet have the skills to fully understand their own struggles, but as you incorporate the strategies in this section, you'll see their confidence bloom. As your child grows older, you can start to bring them more and more into conversations about understanding their challenges and advocating for themselves.

CHALLENGE 1

Self-Esteem and Self-Confidence

The better we feel about ourselves, the more confident we are. The more confident we are, the better able we are to face whatever challenges lie ahead. Confidence and strong feelings of self-esteem or self-worth lead to lowered anxiety, an increased ability to take risks, more resilience, and, ultimately, to an ability to self-advocate for one's needs. The tricky part is knowing how to help your child build that positive self-image so that they can see their own strengths and understand their challenges. Offering praise and encouragement is tantamount, but this will only truly resonate if your child believes it. Your child's self-confidence will take off when they hear you tell them how much you love them. Sounds simple, but knowing you love them shows your child you're in their corner.

That said, a child's sense of self-worth is fragile. While the world of psychology has various viewpoints and interpretations, the overarching theme of a child-parent relationship is that it can have an impact on how that child grows and develops. A caregiver's harsh words said out of frustration can have immense negative effects on the child who hears them. Remember, it is okay to take a deep breath and walk away for a moment.

Helps with

- Boosting self-esteem and building self-confidence

What You'll Need

- Items around the house
- A chore list or chart

When/Where

- Home and outings

Some children are naturally confident and able to walk into any environment and take center stage. Some children need time to warm up in new situations. Some children need to know their advocate is in their corner, and others need more help to recognize and applaud their amazing talents. Before implementing any of the strategies in this section, reflect on your child's emotional development and where they are in owning their self-worth, honoring their self-esteem, and recognizing their own abilities to take on the world. If you feel your child is ready, you can involve them in parts of this reflection as well. Here are some categories and questions to consider:

- General self-perception
  - How comfortable is my child in their own skin?
- My influence on my child
  - How often do I praise my child?
  - Do I provide constructive feedback or criticism?
- Social interactions
  - What sort of friends does my child have?
  - How is my child in new situations?

- Independence and decision-making
    - Can my child do things by themselves?
    - How easily can my child make decisions for themselves?

Model Confidence

Instead of hiding your challenges, let your child see you tackle them with optimism and preparation. Admit to a mistake and share how you'll correct it to show your child that mistakes aren't failures but opportunities to learn. Talk with your child about what it felt like to do something scary, about how you knew you could do it and how you felt so empowered afterward. Most important, always show your child that you love them no matter their challenges. When they know they are supported, they will have the confidence to make the most of new opportunities, even challenging ones.

Build a Growth Mindset

We mentioned in part I that fostering a growth mindset can be a powerful framework for every aspect of life. When we approach our challenges with the belief that our abilities can be improved through learning, effort, and persistence, countless doors open to us. Building positive self-talk takes time. Modeling a growth mindset for your child will show them how to bounce back from challenges.

Here are some things to say when your child is feeling frustrated after what might be perceived as a failure:

- "You've got this, and I believe in you."
- "It's okay. Think about how hard you tried and what you learned from this."

- "I could see that was a little tricky for you but that you were really trying. Imagine how much closer to your goal you are now!"
- "I hear you saying that you don't think you're good at that, but you can try again. What part of that task came easily to you? What's your goal for next time?"
- "That was some great effort! Remember, sometimes you don't win, but you always learn."
- "What can you tell me about this experience?"
- "What's something you did today that you're proud of?"
- "What was the longest thing you read this week? How proud are you that you stuck with it?"

Foster Responsibility

Assign simple chores at home to help your child build responsibility and experience a sense of accomplishment and ownership. The boost in their self-esteem and confidence that comes from doing something all by themselves will leave your child standing a little taller and excitedly sharing about what they were able to do. Moreover, children seek boundaries, want to know what is expected of them, and want to feel like they belong. Understanding how they can pitch in at home helps them understand their place in the family and builds independence.

Here are some simple chores your child might be able to do all by themselves:

- Making their bed
- Cleaning up their toys

- Setting and clearing the table
- Watering plants or feeding pets
- Helping pack their school lunches or prepare their snacks
- Ordering for themselves at a restaurant or drive-through

Tip: Even the most challenging day can feel better with a big hug! Physical touch is a powerful way to regulate the nervous system and can make everything seem better.

CHALLENGE 2

Friendships

Sharing experiences with their friends can be the highlight of any child's school day. That's why kids will always say that recess or lunchtime is their favorite subject. Those positive interactions with peers may be just what your child needs to have the energy to tackle the academic challenges of reading.

Of course, the adults in a child's life are also important. We are there to be their emotional foundation, to model strong social skills and resilience, and to co-regulate and guide. We will talk more about co-regulating later in this chapter, but it means that you are present with your child during moments of frustration or overwhelm. You are there to remain calm yourself and help your child navigate their own emotions.

Making friends can be tricky for some children, especially those who struggle in areas where other children may not. Some children may be shy and uncomfortable engaging with new people. Children with social language difficulties or learning differences may find the task of meeting someone new confusing and daunting. They may not understand what "normal" behavior is or why a peer reacted a certain way to something they did or said.

While dyslexia is a reading challenge, this core struggle can impact how they navigate social settings. Your child with dyslexia may be so overwhelmed by academic requirements that they miss social cues, like a beckoning gesture to join the group. They may feel like their classmates are teasing them or don't accept them because certain academic tasks are difficult. Your child may also start to feel self-conscious about their reading struggles around their peers.

Your role in helping your child build social skills may be larger than you expect. Keep in mind how much influence you have with your child—use your own experiences to show them what good friendships look like, how to navigate new social situations, and how to manage emotions, particularly when difficult feelings may be associated.

Helps with

- Building relationships with classmates and peers

What You'll Need

- A physical reminder such as a chart
- Stuffed animals to act out scenarios

When/Where

- Extracurricular activities
- Playdates

In children between ages six and nine, the foundation of friendships starts to shift. They become more about mutual interests and shared activities than cooperative play (playing the same game or in the same way). Children at this age also start to understand concepts like loyalty and trust, which can deepen the bond with a new friend. As you navigate this new territory with your child, find a balance between encouraging social interactions and respecting your child's wishes. Outgoing children generally find it easier to make friends, while children who are more introverted need more time to form friendships.

Be patient and supportive throughout this journey, understanding that your child's struggles with dyslexia might impact their social interactions. Also, because your child's schedule is likely full as they begin services, managing the logistics of your child's friendships can be difficult. As you practice these strategies, give yourself the grace and space you need to arrange playdates and activities, and remember that unstructured downtime is also important.

Making Connections

When possible, arrange opportunities for your child to make connections with peers outside of school. Playdates and extracurricular activities can give your child the chance to deepen existing friendships and form new ones. While ideally your child would have the chance to initiate interactions in unstructured ways, such as biking with friends in the neighborhood, in today's world, this isn't always possible.

If your child struggles with making new friends, here are some situations that may be easier for them:

Shared activities: Playing games or doing an activity together can break the ice and help children bond.

Structured activities: Team sports can help children mingle in settings with clear boundaries and expectations.

Unstructured play: Free time at the park or in the yard allows kids to negotiate rules, navigate conflicts, and naturally develop social skills.

One-on-one or group settings: Some children may find one-on-one activities more comfortable to initiate connections, while others may find group settings easier.

Provide your child with different opportunities and environments to make connections so that they can practice and adapt the skills they are learning.

Conflict Resolution

Talk with your child about resolving conflicts that may arise on the playground or in other social settings. Friendships often involve disagreements, and children need guidance on how to handle conflict calmly without resorting to aggression or withdrawal. It's also important to help your child understand that disagreements are a normal part of friendships. Good friends mix ideas and make compromises. It's not just about getting what you want all the time.

Your child with dyslexia may have to learn to navigate the extra conflict of being teased in the classroom. They may hear their classmates say things like, "That word is so easy to read! How can you not know it?" or "Why are you so slow to read that?" In these scenarios, encourage your child to respond with "I'm still learning" or "Everyone is different and does things at their own speed."

You can create a chart of options and use stuffed animals to act out scenarios. Here are some choices your child can make when they face conflict:

- Ask them to "please stop."
- Talk it out.
- Take turns.
- Apologize.
- Make a deal.
- Take three deep breaths.
- Walk away and ignore it.

Connect with your child's teacher or intervention team to see if there are any specific frameworks, approaches, or wordings they use regarding conflict resolution. The more consistent you are, the more quickly your child will internalize these skills, leading to independence.

Bullying

Unfortunately, despite everyone's best efforts, bullying is still common, which means that your child may encounter bullying at some point. What's worse is that children with learning disorders are often the target of bullying. Bullying is defined as repeated aggressive behavior with the intention to harm or intimidate another person. Bullying can be physical or verbal and occur one-on-one, in social groups, or online. The key elements of bullying are repetition and intention. This isn't just someone saying something mean once in the hallway or accidentally pushing someone on the playground. This is consistent and with purpose.

Your child's teacher should be on the lookout for bullying, especially around reading. They should inform you of specific instances or patterns of behavior and how they are addressing it at school. This includes calling your child names, mocking your child as they read, excluding your child from activities because they "take too long," and spreading rumors that your child "can't read."

It's important to recognize the signs that your child may be the victim of bullying:

- Suddenly acting differently
- Asking to stay home from school or avoiding a certain activity
- Not wanting to talk about it when asked

If you feel your child is being bullied:

- Let your child know you are there to support them if kids are being mean or excluding them.
- Assure your child that there is nothing to be embarrassed about if kids say mean things.

- Talk to your child's teacher or the adult in charge of the activity for insight and guidance.
- Facilitate conflict resolution, if possible, or request help from a professional.

Tip: Bullying is a much bigger topic than what's covered here. If you ever feel like your child is being teased or bullied, act quickly. Seek professional help if you feel it's necessary, and remove your child from the situation until there's a resolution, if possible.

CHALLENGE 3

Co-Regulation and Emotion Regulation

Our fight-or-flight response can be triggered by anything we perceive as a threat. It doesn't need to be an actual threat to our lives but anything our brains instinctually find menacing—such as reading and schoolwork for your child with dyslexia.

Self-regulation can be defined as when we use the more logical parts of our brain to talk ourselves through reactive feelings. Before a child can practice self-regulating, the process should be demonstrated through co-regulation. Helping your child with dyslexia to cope with big feelings is essential, because their feelings of overwhelm and frustration may be persistent and powerful.

As your child experiences positive moments of co-regulation with you, they'll move closer to being able to self-regulate, which is the ultimate goal. They'll start to internalize the dialogue they have with you, and the grounding strategies you employ together will become more habitual. They'll continue to need you as their emotional foundation and to provide the sense of security that comes with unconditional love, but as their emotion regulation skills improve, you'll see a dip in anxiety and a rise in resilience.

Helps with

- Regulating emotions during difficult moments

What You'll Need

- A crunchy snack, cold water, or chewable jewelry
- Something soft and heavy like a weighted blanket or a stuffed animal

When/Where

- Homework sessions
- Transitions
- Moments of frustration

We are co-regulating when we help a child manage their emotions and/or their body's physical reaction to something that seems scary. You can liken it to taking on the role of the logical part of their brain by providing reassurance and offering comfort and strategies.

As you model and show your child how they can manage their own reactions, you are providing them a road map to absorb and internalize healthy coping skills and strategies. They'll see you regulating your own emotions and learn to identify how they feel when they experience each emotion and how to calm their bodies.

Practice Self-Regulating

Regulating our own emotions as adults is often challenging, let alone for a child. You may get triggered, overstimulated, or have your own reactive feelings when you see your child upset. Co-regulating is a big task for any adult, but it's essential that you're ready to be the calming presence your child needs in difficult moments.

Here are three steps that might help regulate your own emotions:

1. Learn to recognize your own emotional state. When do you feel calm and prepared? When do you feel frustrated or angry? What triggers you to go from one state to another?

2. Identify techniques that help you transition from frustrated back to calm. For example, take three deep breaths and feel your body calm with each one, count to 10 in your head to give yourself a pause before reacting, remember a positive memory like a vacation or time with friends, or do a mindfulness trick like squeezing your fists or shoulder raises. These can all help release anger or tension and bring you back to a calm state. Practice your chosen calming techniques until they become second nature.

3. Remind yourself that it is okay to become upset, but it's crucial to be the emotional rock your child needs during hard moments.

Talk about Emotions

Talk about your child's emotional response—but never in the moment. When we are in an unregulated state, our prefrontal cortex can be flooded with stress hormones, so we may be incapable of thinking logically. This can be especially true for children, whose brains are still developing.

When we experience an emotion, there are often physical signs in the rest of our body as well. Find calm, quiet times to talk about big feelings and what our bodies feel like when we are experiencing these emotions. This can look and sound like:

- Making different faces to represent a feeling and asking what happens to the rest of their body when their face looks like that. For example:
  - For anger, maybe their stomach hurts or their head feels heavy.
  - For happiness, maybe their whole body feels light.

Avoid letting the moment escalate. Remember that when your child is in the middle of feeling a big emotion, they may be incapable of listening to you and may need to return to a calmer state before processing what you're saying.

Rating the Reaction and the Problem

Whenever your child seems to have a bigger than expected reaction to something, like if they start to cry because the store was out of their favorite ice cream flavor, talk about how you can compare the problem with the reaction. To them, it might feel like the end of the world, but with practice, they can begin to recognize if their reaction is a match or a mismatch. You can do this by using a scale of one to five to rate the problem and the reaction. Help your child see if the numbers match or if they're maybe overreacting to what just happened.

Using an even, unemotional tone to co-regulate with your child, try these scripts to guide them in recognizing their unexpected response during a tense moment:

> "I see you're upset right now. It looks to me like your reaction is a four. What problem caused you to become upset? What size problem was it?"
>
> "I'd rate that problem a two. It seems to me that your reaction is *un*expected and is a *mis*match with the size of the problem. Let's try having a matched reaction."

> "Let's try some of the breathing exercises we practiced last weekend so that our reaction matches the size of the problem."

Introduce this concept when your child is regulated, and model this thinking process with your own problems as well.

Tip: Take time for yourself as often as possible so that you can better support your child emotionally when your child needs you. Make sure to learn about your own emotional state and how to recognize signs that your reserves are depleting.

CHALLENGE 4

Anxiety

Unfortunately, anxiety is increasing in all age groups, including young children. Your child with dyslexia may have difficulty with anxiety due to their dyslexia-related struggles. In fact, some studies show that as many as 50 percent of people with dyslexia experience anxiety.

While both are a natural response, anxiety and stress have distinct differences. Anxiety is often more internalized, characterized by an overwhelming or excessive sense of worry. While stress may come and go based on the situation or as a reaction to external factors, anxiety is persistent, even if the person "knows there is nothing wrong" or wants to relax.

Anxiety can present differently in different people. There are also different types and causes of anxiety, and some people may be more prone to anxiety in the first place. Anxiety can also be influenced by environmental factors. For your child with dyslexia, their anxiety may be related to specific moments or settings, such as:

- Academic environments or performance
- Moments of separation
- Certain social interactions

Helps with

- Recognizing and lowering anxiety

What You'll Need

- A favorite stuffed animal or soothing toy

When/Where

- At home or any quiet, safe place
- Whenever your child is feeling anxious

Some children with anxiety may appear nervous or distracted, while others may become quiet and withdrawn. Some children may even become selectively mute. Selective mutism is when an individual is capable of speaking, but they may refuse or be unable to speak.

Some children may not be able to openly express their feelings of anxiety, so here are some signs to look for in your child:

- Constant complaints of aches and pains, particularly stomachaches or headaches
- Changes in their behavior or appetite
- Refusing to participate in daily activities or go to school
- Trouble going to sleep or staying asleep

If your child's anxiety is persistent, work with a qualified mental health professional who can support your child in reducing their anxiety. While feeling stressed during tense moments is normal, prolonged feelings of anxiety are not.

On the topic of anxiety, I would feel remiss if I didn't discuss the role technology can have on a child's social and emotional development. I encourage you to wait to get your child their own smartphone—scrolling social media and navigating text chains can increase anxiety. For more on this, read *The Anxious Generation* by Jonathan Haidt.

Practice Mindfulness

Find fun, authentic ways to practice mindfulness with your child. Mindfulness is the state of being aware of your own thoughts and feelings and the world around you, without judgment and with complete acceptance. When we incorporate mindfulness as a way of viewing the world and your own mind, we can see it as more than just a current trend.

Here are a few fun ways to practice mindfulness with your child:

Bubble breaths: Take a deep breath and pretend you are blowing bubbles. This helps children focus on their breathing, which can reset the nervous system.

The listening game: Close your eyes and name all the sounds you can hear.

Gratitude practices: Take time as a family to share what you are grateful for about each other.

Identify Triggers

Observe and work with your child to identify their triggers. When we are aware of situations and events that can start an unwanted emotional reaction, it can help us be better prepared to regulate ourselves through any difficult feelings that might arise. This doesn't mean we should avoid those situations, as it is important to face challenges, but you can be ready to help co-regulate with your child if needed.

For your child with dyslexia, it's also important to remember that reading itself may be a trigger, especially when they are first starting their intervention program. Here are some other things to consider when looking for the patterns of your child's potential triggers:

- Certain times of day
- Specific locations or events
- Difficult tasks or circumstances
- Physical needs like hunger or feeling tired

The 3-3-3 Rule

The 3-3-3 rule is a way for your child to calm their anxiety by focusing on the world around them to bring them back to the present moment. Teach them this strategy during regulated moments and model how it can look. Then, during a triggering moment, you can guide them through the strategy. With practice, they can independently apply the strategy whenever they're feeling an increase in anxiety.

Here are the steps to help your child's mind move through the overwhelming sensation:

1. Name three objects around you.
2. Name three sounds you hear.
3. Move three parts of your body.

Tip: Adapt these strategies to best fit your child's unique needs. With the 3-3-3 rule, for example, some children may need more guidelines. They may want to name three colors or three living things instead of simply any object they see.

CHALLENGE 5

Self-Advocacy

Common tasks in schools may be more difficult for your child. They may need extended time to complete assignments, or they may need alternative ways to demonstrate their knowledge. These struggles may extend beyond their academic journey into work settings or adult activities. To successfully navigate all of that, your child needs to know how to advocate for themselves.

Self-advocacy is the ability to understand and communicate your own needs in a way that makes sense to others to hopefully receive the support you need. It's being able to share the cause of your challenge and clearly explain what you need to be successful with whatever you're being asked to do. You understand what you need, and you can ask for help. It takes knowledge and courage to self-advocate, though, so supporting your child in learning how to advocate for themselves from a young age will set them up for success.

Here are some things to keep in mind about self-advocacy. Self-advocacy must be:

- Respectful
- Honest
- Proactive
- Empowering

For others to hear what your child is saying, they need to learn how to:

- Explain things in a way others can understand.
- Use a positive tone of voice.
- Be consistent.
- Be polite, yet firm.
- Plan ahead.
- Find the right person to communicate with.

You can practice these skills with your child not only regarding dyslexia but also generally as they navigate their day. Seeing you successfully self-advocate is a powerful way for your child to learn how to successfully advocate for themselves.

Helps with

- Building self-advocacy skills

What You'll Need

- Nothing

When/Where

- Conversations with your child
- Conversations with teachers

In the elementary school years, self-advocacy is more about your child understanding their dyslexia and what that means for them as learners. They may start to learn how to share with new teachers about their learning differences and what that means for them in the classroom. They can also learn how to communicate with their teachers about how certain assignments might be more difficult for them and what alternatives or accommodations they may need to succeed.

As they grow older, your child can learn more about their legal rights and the accommodations they are eligible for. In high school, they can learn about the requirements for accommodations with standardized testing and the process to ensure they receive additional time or other necessary accommodations. If your child is on the path to attend college, they can learn how to navigate the student support system at their new campus and how to get in touch with professors. These are all thoughts for down the road, but you're laying the foundation for your child's success by starting simple and early with these strategies.

Describe Their Dyslexia

Help your child first understand what dyslexia is and what it means for them. This is a conversation that may be difficult, but talking about your child's diagnosis with them will help them better understand themselves and be empowered to share with others. If you have not yet shared their diagnosis with them, see page 51 for a script.

Help your child learn how to describe their learning challenges in a calm and affirming setting. Here are some considerations:

- Pick the right time and place when your child seems receptive.
- Be positive and affirming. Remind your child that we are all different and that is what makes each of us special.

- Discuss dyslexia in language your child will understand. Revisit what you told your child when you shared their diagnosis with them.

Once your child understands their dyslexia and knows what their unique challenges are, they can practice sharing this information with new teachers or friends. Here is something that your child may feel comfortable saying: "I have dyslexia. This means my reading brain works in a different way."

Identify Their Needs

Help your child identify their needs and practice sharing them with their teachers. Here are a few sharing statements your child may feel comfortable saying:

> "My dyslexia means that I need more time to read what you give me. It means that I need more time to write down my thoughts and that my spelling may not be correct."
>
> "I know you want me to learn about (*insert topic*), but reading that book is going to be really hard for me. Can I listen to it instead, please?"

Ask for Help

Guide your child in knowing when to ask for help. Nobody needs to do it all alone, especially a child with dyslexia. Role-play what the conversation with a teacher might sound like. Here's a sample script:

> Your child: "I need help writing down my thoughts."
>
> Teacher: "I understand, but you need to do it by yourself."

> Your child: "I have dyslexia, so this is harder for me than you might think it is. Can I use the iPad to record my voice, please?"

Tip: Learning to respectfully and proactively self-advocate is a lifelong practice. It's normal for your child to initially be hesitant to share this information. Remain supportive and give your child time to process sharing.

If Your Child Needs More Support

This chapter is a surface-level overview of the social and emotional challenges your child with dyslexia might face. The strategies included here should help, but there's more involved. If these strategies aren't enough or you are beyond your capacity to help your child, seek help from the right professionals. Don't wait, as your child's self-esteem and self-confidence may be more fragile than you realize.

Here's a list of the different types of mental health professionals to consider:

Child psychologist: a mental health professional who specializes in the development of children and adolescents; they may diagnose and/or treat

Child psychiatrist: a doctor who attended medical school and pursued additional training to specialize in mental health disorders in children and adolescents; they may diagnose and/or prescribe medication

Licensed clinical social worker: a licensed mental health professional with a master's degree in social work who works with children and families

Licensed professional counselor: a licensed mental health professional who provides therapy

School counselor: a licensed professional who works within schools to support students with emotional well-being and academic concerns

Play therapist: a trained and certified professional who uses play as a therapeutic tool for helping children express themselves and work through challenges

Neurofeedback specialist: neurofeedback may be provided by a psychologist, licensed counselor, licensed therapist, medical professional, and/or certified neurofeedback specialist. Neurofeedback provides real-time information on brain activity and can be used to address patterns.

Art or music therapist: a trained and certified professional who uses creative expression to help people improve their well-being

Equine specialist in mental health and learning: a trained and certified professional who uses horses to help people improve their mental health, well-being, and capacity to learn

Do your homework before committing to working with anyone. In addition to using your intuition to decide whether this person feels like the right fit for your child, here are some questions to ask:

- What is your training and what credentials do you hold?
- Are you licensed in my state or country to provide the services you are offering?
- What is your experience with children? What is your experience with children with learning differences?
- What is your approach? What techniques do you use?
- How likely are you to connect with my child?
- What communication can I expect from you?

Reflection

Social and emotional development takes time, and you may likely witness ups and downs with your child—and with yourself. As you begin to use the strategies in this chapter, reflect on the growth you've seen in your child and with your family as a whole. Use the following guiding questions to consider the progress you've made and how you can continue to support your child with dyslexia:

What strategies have you tried?

____

____

____

____

What successes can you celebrate? Have there been any small moments when you saw your child make a connection with a peer, take a deep breath and relax, better articulate their needs, or bounce back from a small stumble?

____

____

____

____

Were there moments in your child's day when they struggled with emotions or social interactions? How did they respond, and how did you support them? What worked well, and what might you try differently next time?

If you zoom out and take a bird's-eye view of your child's social and emotional development, are you seeing a broad trend toward progress?

6

Cognitive and Other Academic Skills

As your child moves through their school day, their dyslexia will make tasks harder. Not only will learning to read be a hurdle, but it can drain their mental battery, leaving them with less energy to tackle everything else they're asked to do. If your child is facing any coexisting challenges, they may have other hurdles such as completing class assignments, organizing their materials for class, processing information quickly enough to keep up with the teacher, following multistep instructions, or staying engaged during discussions. This chapter breaks all this down and helps you practice skills with your child to make it easier for them to navigate their school day.

Common Challenge Areas

Cognitive development in children is a process that continues through the mid-20s, at which point the brain is fully developed, according to research, but changes can still take place after that. As they age, almost all children learn how to:

- Think for themselves.
- Remember things.

- Make sense of the world around them.
- Logically process information.

The development of these skills may take more time for your child with dyslexia. In part I, we covered three cognitive functions: working memory, processing speed, and executive functioning skills. For a refresher, refer to pages 43 and 44. When it comes to the term "executive functioning skills," you may often hear it used regarding children with ADHD; that's because there's usually a notable deficit in this area. But executive functioning deficits aren't limited to ADHD.

In a nutshell, executive functioning skills are the set of skills we use to:

- Initiate a task.
- Maintain focus on something.
- Switch tasks.
- Decide how much effort to exert.
- Regulate our emotions and behaviors.
- Effectively use our memory.
- Plan ahead.

What do executive functioning skills look like in real life? They help us get out the door on time with everything we need for the day. They help us plan ahead, multitask, make quick decisions, and stay on track during a conversation. For your child, these skills help them make sure their backpack is ready for school, keep them engaged when their teacher is talking, see a project through to completion, know which direction they need to go to get to their locker, and so on. In fact, any time we set out to do something and then do it successfully, we rely on our executive functioning skills.

Children struggle with these steps in general because of where they are in their cognitive development. What's more, children do not develop an understanding of how long five minutes or an hour actually takes until around age six or seven. It's not until they reach age eight or nine that more abstract concepts of time make sense, such as how long a month is. All children struggle with time management and prioritizing tasks, not just children with deficits in this area.

Whether or not your child has executive functioning deficits, they can certainly strengthen their skills with practice, and because of their dyslexia and its challenges, some of these detailed tasks might be a little bit tougher. Now's the time to anchor the support your child needs to learn how to be more independent in these areas. As they grow older, they will be required to navigate the school day more independently, keep track of their own schedule, and remember how to be prepared. You can help set them up for success.

CHALLENGE 1

Daily Routines

Understanding how long things take, managing time accordingly, understanding the steps required, and sticking to a plan are all key elements in successfully navigating a daily routine. For any child between the ages of six and nine, this is difficult: Their concept of time isn't fully developed, they may not be able to envision the final step of the process, or may not know each individual task required to get there—yet. It's possible, though, that their brains just aren't ready for that level of independence—yet. Because of this, they may need consistent reminders to stay on track. Your child with dyslexia may struggle even more, especially if they are navigating other challenges.

If you consistently apply the strategies in this section, your child should learn to better manage their daily routines, avoiding mishaps and achieving the outcome they're after.

Helps with

- Independently completing daily tasks and routines

What You'll Need

- Visual schedule
- Sand or kitchen timers
- Daily planner

When/Where

- Daily activities at home

We all thrive on consistency, but children with learning differences do even more so. The more consistent expectations and routines are, the more quickly they can move toward independently completing tasks. They don't have to spend time and energy wondering what is expected of them or trying to figure out what they're supposed to do next. They can focus on doing what they know they need to do.

The clearer you can help your child plan out their day in consistent, manageable chunks, the easier it will be for everyone. They will know what to expect and what they need to accomplish, and you can hopefully move away from persistent reminders to the occasional prompt or cue. It will take time for them to learn their new routines, and they will likely still need help when mishaps arise.

Visual Schedule

Work with your child to create a visual schedule of their day. You can create different schedules for different parts of their day. Every family is different, but the three typical tricky times are getting ready in the morning, coming home from school, and getting ready for bed. When you're chatting with your child about making their schedule with them, don't try to think of every tiny detail; instead, focus on the flow of the schedule. Once you have the main pieces in mind, discuss with your child why they're important and what order they need to happen in. For example, do they eat breakfast first and then brush their teeth?

Here are some tips to help you get started:

Dos

- Talk with your child about what you're creating together and why.
- Take a quiet morning, like on the weekend, to walk through their morning routine of what they must do before leaving for school.
- Use *real* photos of them completing the tasks.
- Make it manageable.
- Be consistent.
- Keep it simple.

Don'ts

- Avoid using clip art or just words since reading steps may be too much for them when they're first beginning intervention. Also, using real pictures gives your child the mental image that they may be struggling to come up with on their own.
- Try not to create a schedule if you're already busy.
- Try not to be judgmental.
- Try not to make things overly complicated; keep it simple.

Understanding Time

Find fun ways throughout your day to help your child develop their concept of the passage of time. Here are some easy things you can do together:

- Time the drive to school.
- Notice how long a TV episode is before you watch it together, and then, when it's over, remind your child how long it was.
- Use a timer for them to practice brushing their teeth for two minutes.
- Set a timer when you're cooking or baking together.

Daily Planners

Help your child set up a daily planner to keep track of school assignments and extracurricular activities. Check with your child's school, as they may already have one that you can also use.

Set regular times to sit down with your child each day and look ahead at what they have on their plate that week. Talk through how to "plan backward" to manage tasks and their time. Planning backward means you start by discussing the goal and then work through the steps in reverse. Here's a sample script:

> "I see that you have a big event on Saturday. Can you tell me about it?"
>
> *Your child replies by telling you about their upcoming gymnastics competition.*
>
> "I know Saturday mornings can be busy because we're not following our usual routines. I also know that your sister has an activity that morning, too. How can we make sure we're prepared for your big competition?"
>
> *You and your child brainstorm ways to prepare.*
>
> "We have some free time now. Let's get your uniform ready so Saturday morning will be easier."
>
> *You and your child get their equipment together.*

Tip: If you're looking for more resources to support your child's daily routines, check out the website for Cognitive Connections listed in the resources section on page 231. And remember that an occasional deviation from your child's schedule encourages flexibility and resilience!

CHALLENGE 2

Organization and Memory

Being organized requires a combination of skills, including well-developed executive functioning skills and a good memory. Organized individuals take time to plan ahead, organize their spaces, and create habits that set them up for success. Executive functioning skills help us stay organized because they give us the ability to:

- See ahead.
- Identify what is needed to complete a task.
- Make a plan to complete the task.
- Execute the plan.

Memory plays a large role in being organized because:

- We need to remember facts and how to do things.
- We need to be able to hold on to information we're currently processing.
- We need to utilize the brain's whiteboard to manipulate all the information.

To navigate their school day, your child needs to be able to do all of that, especially as they move to third grade and beyond. It's extra important for your child with dyslexia to be organized because they'll likely face frustrations throughout their day, and the smoother their day, the more brainpower and emotional bandwidth they'll have to remain resilient and focused.

Being organized also comes down to good habits. Organized spaces mean fewer lost moments searching for something. Journals and lists help move tasks out of working memory and onto something concrete, while schedules help us manage our time and stay on track. Yes, getting and staying organized requires effort. While it's easier for some than others, you can model these healthy habits and help your child develop them as well.

Helps with

- Being organized and remembering to bring what is needed

What You'll Need

- Pictures of your child ready to go
- Baskets and hooks to use for organizing

When/Where

- Daily activities at home

Getting and staying organized can be even more difficult for your child with dyslexia if they also have some challenges in their executive functioning skills and working memory. But no matter their level of difficulty, the strategies in this section can support their ability to stay organized and remember important details, like where something is or what they need to do next. As your child grows and becomes more self-aware, help them recognize the value in organization and share your own experience as an example. In my case, designating a spot in my house for my keys made my whole life easier!

Make the Final Picture Clear

Help your child visualize the final picture—it can be the desired outcome of what they need to do or where they ultimately need to land. This kick-starts their brain's ability to plan for, break down, start, and finish a task. Create a framework to help them see what it will look like when they have everything they need and are ready to go.

A common challenge is getting ready to leave the house in the morning, so we'll use it as an example, but you can tailor this to any desired outcome. To help your child visualize the final product of walking out the door, follow these steps:

1. Have your child get dressed and ready as if they are going to school.
2. Have them stand by the door with the right clothes on, their backpack in hand, and everything else they need.
3. Take their picture.
4. Print the picture.
5. Use a marker to circle the key items they need.

Your child can then refer to this photo when getting ready.

Create Categories

Use the picture you created in the previous strategy to put together categories of items your child needs at different points of their day and week. Take more pictures to help them visualize and remember the different items for each category. For example, in step 2 above, they needed their backpack. Break this down further by taking these steps:

1. Ask your child to lay out everything that needs to go into their backpack.
2. Take a picture.
3. Print the picture.

You can repeat this strategy for after-school activities, trips to visit their grandparents, or anything your child does frequently.

Organize the Space

Use bags, baskets, and hooks to keep categories of items together. Use the pictures you created in the two earlier approaches as labels for the baskets. Whenever your child comes home from an activity, have them put everything in the basket so that it's all ready to go next time.

If there are things that need to be washed, work with your child to set routines to replace everything in the baskets once they're washed and ready to be used again.

Tip: Finding the space to keep everything organized can be a challenge, especially if you're living in a small space or have a large family. Use your vertical space to get and stay organized. You can find plastic stools your child can use to reach higher spaces.

CHALLENGE 3

Making Decisions

You're probably aware of how many factors go into making your decisions in life, big and small, especially when it comes to helping your child with dyslexia succeed. Sometimes, you may find all this decision-making a bit overwhelming. Now imagine the task of decision-making for your child with dyslexia. It might range from overwhelming to almost impossible.

A seemingly simple question like, "What do you want for dinner?" has many layers to it. Your child needs to think about how hungry they are, sort through the options of what they like to eat, reflect on what might be feasible for dinner, pause and look ahead at what your reaction might be, and then decide. Finally, they have to verbalize all that. That's a lot to consider, so try to remember that what you might consider an easy decision to make might be frustrating for your child, and what you find frustrating might feel impossible to them.

Helps with:

- Learning how to make decisions

What You'll Need

- Nothing

When/Where

- Home
- Conversations with your child

To help your child build their critical-thinking and decision-making skills, give them the opportunity to make choices for themselves when decisions are low-stakes. Many children with dyslexia feel powerless during their school day, but you can incorporate easy decisions to help them feel in control of their day. This is also good practice for making tougher decisions later and gives you valuable opportunities to have conversations with your child about what is important to them. Weekends and holidays are good times to let them pick out their own clothes or choose their own snacks, when there is no time pressure to their decision-making process. You can also talk through bigger decisions like what sport they might want to play next season or what gift they want to get their family member or friend for their birthday. The strategies in this section will guide you to help them be better decision-makers.

Clearly Make a Request

I've stressed the value of open-ended questions as a way to engage your child in conversations and learn about their emotions, so this approach might seem a little contradictory. But it's for good reason under very specific circumstances.

Sometimes you'll need your child to do something you know they may be reluctant to do. For your child with dyslexia, homework and reading will likely be among things they don't want to do. For a child facing other challenges, they might not want to sit down for a meal, transition from one place to another, or stop a favorite activity. In these instances, it's important to be kind, but clear, as their only decision is to comply.

That means, whenever those instances come up, avoid asking questions that can be answered with a yes or no. We often think we're being polite by asking a question, when in reality we're making a statement or giving a command. When we communicate with children this way, it causes confusion on their end and frustration on ours.

Instead of saying . . .	Say . . .
"Are you ready to go?"	"It's time to go. Please meet me at the garage now."
"Do you want dinner now?"	"Dinner will be ready in five minutes. Wash your hands and come sit down."
"Did you finish your homework?"	"I know you have homework today. Let's look at your folder together."

Provide Two Choices

There may be moments when your child needs to complete something. They can still have a voice in the process. These times are when you can give your child options that respect their input without being a potentially frustrating open-ended decision. When you need to ask your child to make a decision, provide two choices and ask which they prefer. Stick to your options and repeat them if needed and avoid letting the process become a negotiation. If your child can't make the decision at the moment, let them know that you'll choose for them. Here's a sample script to illustrate how you might ask your child to make a decision:

> You: "Would you like carrot sticks or broccoli with your dinner?"
>
> Child: "I don't want either."
>
> You: "That's not a choice. Would you like carrot sticks or broccoli with your dinner? They are both good. Please make a choice, or I'll choose for you."

Use Natural Incentives to Encourage Reading and Homework Time

When you're motivating your child to make a choice to read without complaint, focus on natural incentives rather than repeated warnings. Some people believe that multiple reminders help children make better choices, while others suggest they may become overly reliant on them, reducing the learning opportunity that comes with natural incentives and consequences.

There are times when giving a heads-up is helpful for your child, like preparing for a transition. This can sound like, "In ten minutes, we'll switch to reading time." But the idea here is to use natural incentives instead of reminders or warnings. Here are two things to keep in mind:

Set clear expectations. Use the other strategies in this chapter to set a daily schedule so that your child knows when reading time is, and share with your child why reading is so important.

Check in with your child. Sometimes your child is not emotionally ready to transition to a tricky task like reading. If that's the case, use the co-regulating strategies you learned in chapter 5 before transitioning.

The table below presents a few ideas for using natural incentives to promote reading and homework time.

Scenario	Natural Incentives
Reading time	• Choose a favorite snack to munch on while reading. • Find a book on a topic they love. • Allow your child to reread an old favorite once or twice a week. • Read in a cozy spot or a favorite park.
Math homework	• Let them choose the order of the problems to complete. • Make a connection to a real-world situation. • Let them be the teacher and show a family member or stuffed animal how to do it.
Larger project like a science fair poster	• Break up the project into manageable chunks so your child can see their progress. • Have a dance break after completing each piece of the project. • Big projects deserve big celebrations, so have a special treat or share a special moment when they're all finished.

Tip: With continued practice, your child will learn the difference between when they need to do what you ask and when they can make a choice.

CHALLENGE 4

Sequencing Skills

When we put things in a specific order, we are sequencing them. This can range from everyday tasks like making a peanut butter and jelly sandwich to academic tasks like writing a story. Regardless of the context, sequencing allows us to put steps, items, or concepts into the correct, logical order.

Like many of the skills we've discussed, being able to successfully sequence is the culmination of different skills. Let's look at a real-world example and an academic one that your child might be asked to do and walk through what is needed to complete each.

Real-world example: Making a peanut butter and jelly sandwich

1. Buy or gather all the needed materials.
2. Open all containers.
3. Get two knives.
4. Spread the peanut butter on one slice of bread.
5. Spread the jelly on the other slice of bread.
6. Combine the two slices to make a sandwich.
7. Enjoy!

Academic example: Writing a story

1. Understand the assignment.
2. Come up with a story with characters, a setting, and a clear plot.
3. Write the beginning of the story.
4. Write the middle of the story.
5. Write the end of the story.
6. Revise the story to make sure it makes sense and includes all the details the teacher wants to see.
7. Edit the story for capitalization, punctuation, and spelling.
8. Turn the story in to the teacher.

Even listing the steps can seem overwhelming, and we didn't even break apart each of the actual tasks. Just think of all the individual steps you must do to prepare the ingredients for the sandwich. Are you making everything from scratch or buying sliced bread? For the story, the second step, coming up with your own story, can already seem enormous, let alone the myriad things the child needs to do after that.

All of this is to say that seeing the result and logically working backward through the steps to sequence them is a big ask for anyone, and even more so for a child who is still growing and learning with dyslexia.

Helps with:

- Knowing how to sequence daily tasks and stories

What You'll Need

- Story cards
- Kitchen items

When/Where

- Home
- Out and about with your child

Any child between the ages of six and nine is learning how to think logically and make sense of the world around them. This includes knowing how to put things in the right order and break apart larger tasks into smaller steps. This also crosses over into their reading and writing, which requires a lot of logical thinking, like sequencing.

For a child with dyslexia, understanding what they read will likely be challenging. For a child with other learning differences in addition to their dyslexia, logical thinking itself may be challenging. This means that retelling stories and organizing their thoughts for writing may be more difficult for them. These strategies can help them build logical thinking and sequencing skills. Growing these skills through non-reading activities will translate to their reading and writing as those skills develop as well. With the right teaching, correct practice, and time, they will develop sequencing skills, which will help them be competent readers and writers.

Model Sequencing

When you have time and it's appropriate, share your sequencing skills with your child through daily examples. For example:

- As you are packing the car for a trip, talk with your child about why you put the big pieces of luggage in first.
- If you're cleaning the house together, talk about why you might dust before vacuuming.

Try not to make these moments into official lessons. Simply sharing what's going through your mind as you are sequencing things and thinking logically will provide concrete examples for your child to model.

Story Cards

Create your own story cards by cutting pictures out of magazines and pasting them on cardboard. Be sure that the pictures are in a certain order to tell a story. Use the cards to practice sequencing and oral storytelling. If you don't want to make your own cards, a variety of story cards are available for purchase or for free online.

Here are the steps to follow:

1. Lay the cards out in a random order.
2. Ask your child, "Which do you think would go first? Where does the story begin? Why do you think that?"
3. Once your child chooses a card, ask them questions like, "What's happening in this picture? What characters do you see?" Refer to the question prompts from chapter 4 on page 118 for more ideas.

4. Continue putting the cards in order. Remember that there may be more than one way to put the cards together, as long as the story is sequential and makes sense.

5. Take a video of your child sharing the story to help them feel like a true storyteller. Plus, the video offers lots of ways to extend your child's learning, such as:
   - Rewatch the story and see what details you want to change.
   - Rewatch the story to see if there are any words your child wants to swap for new vocabulary words.
   - Retell the story with different endings and then talk about how they're similar and different.
   - Create a viewing party with family and friends to celebrate your child's story.
   - Work with your child to write down their words; they can even create a book of their own.

Cooking Together

Have fun preparing food with your child. Keep it as simple as you'd like. The process of cooking or putting together premade meals or setting and clearing the table requires your child to visualize the final image of sitting down to eat with you and working backward through the steps.

Here are a few things to keep in mind:

- Keep your child safe in the kitchen by teaching them how to handle knives and other dangerous items.

- Even if you're not one to cook, prepare sandwiches or bagged salads together. Have your child set the table or get the condiments from the refrigerator.
- Share your thinking with your child as you talk through everything you'll need for the meal.

Tip: If your child is struggling to sequence a story, there may be other reasons for their struggles. Language or other cognitive skill deficits could be impacting their development, and it might be time to see a speech language pathologist or a psychologist for help.

CHALLENGE 5

Attention and Engagement

"Paying attention" is a mix of initiating and sustaining focus and remaining engaged despite external stimuli. It also helps if it's something we want to do and not just something we have to do. Let's talk a little more about the different kinds of attention.

Psychologists have determined that there are different kinds of attention. The table below shows some examples. All are necessary during our daily lives, and they are even more important in academic settings.

Think about how many of these kinds of attention you use in your personal and professional lives. Now think of how many kinds of attention your child needs to successfully complete a day at school. If you feel comfortable, include your child in the discussion.

Helps with:

- Building stamina in remaining engaged and completing tasks

What You'll Need

- Schedules
- Sand or kitchen timers
- High-interest books

When/Where

- Home
- Out and about with your child

Type of Attention	Being Able to . . .	Real-World Example
Focused	Focus on one thing while ignoring everything else	Reading your shopping list in a crowded, noisy grocery store
Sustained	Remain focused on one thing over a long period of time	Staying present and listening during a long meeting
Divided	Multitask, or stay focused on completing different tasks at seemingly the same time	Checking emails while cooking dinner
Alternating	Shift focus between multiple tasks that require more attention	Switching tabs on your computer to jump between checking emails and reading the news
Executive	Manage and control other cognitive processes like thinking logically, analyzing, or planning	Creating a blocked schedule for the day based on your current to-do list

All children will struggle with attention and engagement. Their age can provide a good rule of thumb for what to expect as far as focused attention. A basic formula to follow is:

(age) x 2 = the number of minutes they can be expected to focus on something tricky or really pay attention

After a break of three to 10 minutes, they are probably ready for that same amount of time again. They may be able to repeat that cycle a few times before they need a longer break.

This may be different for your child. Dyslexia is not an attention-deficit disorder, but knowing that something is going to be hard might make your child not even want to start. For a child who also has executive functioning deficits, getting started on something undesirable can be a challenge, and sticking with it until completion may be almost impossible. With your help and these strategies, your child can learn to "pay attention" and finish difficult things.

Have Fun to Make Structure Sustainable

This strategy expands on creating a daily schedule by making it more engaging for your child while helping them pay attention and finish their must-do tasks. Your child's personal daily schedule should include everything they need to do independently, such as putting away their clothing, finishing their homework, and packing their backpack for the next morning. To add some fun to these tasks, consider these ideas:

- Turn routines into role-play opportunities, like being chefs in a fancy restaurant at dinnertime, dentists when they're brushing their teeth, or hotel staff or guests when they're tidying up their room.
- Create playlists with your child for different parts of their routine. You can choose different rhythms or styles of music depending on the mood you want to set.
- Have your child come up with a fun handshake to signal the end of a task.

You Must Do, You Can Do

There are some things your child must do and some they can do. Explain to your child that they need to finish what they must do before they can move on to the optional activities.

Create a chart using photos or pictures to clearly demonstrate which are "must dos" and which are "can dos."

If your child is struggling with staying focused on the required tasks, here are some sample scripts:

> "Playing with that toy is not a choice right now. First, you must pack your backpack."
>
> "Using the iPad is not an option. You need to brush your teeth first."

If you notice that your child has an unexpectedly large reaction to your request, refer to the co-regulating strategies you learned in chapter 5.

High-Interest Options

Use what you know about your child and talk with them about what they're interested in to find options that speak to them. For example, if your child likes to create things, get a few different types of art media for them to choose from. Providing high-interest options is especially important when choosing books for your child with dyslexia to read independently. Check out publishers like High Noon Books, listed in the resources section on page 231, which specializes in books for all maturity levels, but at lower reading levels. They have great decodable chapter books that help your child feel like they're reading more challenging material without feeling frustrated.

> **Tip:** Every child shows signs of inattention, hyperactivity, or impulsivity. If you ever feel that your child's inattention is causing harm, though, either physically or emotionally, seek help from your pediatrician, a psychologist, or a psychiatrist.

Advocate for Accommodations

The more you know about how the school system works, the more empowered you'll be to support and advocate for your child. You can utilize these advocating tips not only for assessments, but also more broadly for what your child needs to be successful at school. Remembering that it may look different from school to school, here are general steps and tips to consider:

1. Review the services and accommodations listed in your child's psychoeducational report.
2. Find out which of these services and accommodations your child's school can offer. Here's a quick list of what you definitely want your child to receive if offered by the school:
   - High-quality dyslexia intervention
   - Extra time on exams
   - Preferential seating
   - Appropriate technology accommodations
3. Compare what your child needs with what the school offers.
4. Know your rights. Visit Wrightslaw at wrightslaw.com to see what the law is in your state.
5. Find out what sort of plan your child has at the school. Is it an IEP, a 504 plan, or something specific to the school?
6. Advocate for your child to receive services and accommodations.
   - Be prepared for meetings by bringing samples, updates, observations, and feedback from teachers and your child's interventionist.
   - Keep a record of all your meetings and conversations.

- Always put your communication in writing to document what you've asked for.
- Even if you have an in-person conversation, send a follow-up email.
- Consider bringing an interventionist, advocate, or other professional to a meeting if needed.

Here is a script you might find helpful:

> "To help (*child's name*) succeed, I am requesting (IEP/504) accommodations based on their learning needs. I am requesting (*accommodations*), which are outlined in the recommendations of their psychoeducational report."

At the end of the day, the more you know, the more you can communicate politely yet firmly, and the more you're prepared, the more support your child will receive. It seems like a lot, but your child deserves to receive the services and accommodations listed and you are their voice. You can do this!

Reflection

As with every category of challenges, it will take time for your child's cognitive and executive functioning skills to develop and it may take time to learn where your child's strengths and areas of improvement are. As you implement the strategies you've learned, reflect on how they're helping your child and your family. Here are some questions to guide your thinking:

What strategies have you tried?

____

____

____

How consistent have you been with using these strategies?

____

____

____

How open has your child been to trying new things to support their independence? Are they ready for these strategies or is there work you need to do to help them be more ready to try them?

____

____

____

____

Even if it's been small, what successes have you seen? What wins can you celebrate?

Are you feeling a downward trend in the number of times you need to prompt your child?

Have you felt a calmer rhythm to your days at home?

What goals do you still have for your child's development?

Is there anything you need to communicate to your child's school?

Are you feeling confident implementing these strategies or do you need more support?

7

Sensory and Motor Integration

We know that dyslexia is a word-level reading challenge, so you may think that challenges with sensory and motor integration don't apply to your child. Sure, if we look just at the definition of dyslexia, they don't. However, experience has shown me that these are common challenges for children with learning differences, and it's important to give you the most complete picture I can. No matter your child's challenges, the strategies in this chapter will help your child's overall development and support their learning process.

Common Challenge Areas

We experience and move through our world with our senses and motor responses. Our brain helps us do all of this. It receives information from our environment and our interactions with our surroundings. It then integrates and processes these stimuli before deciding how we're going to respond. For children, all these individual processes are still developing. You may notice that your child with dyslexia might be somewhat behind their peers and want to know how to help.

Sensory Integration

Did you know there are two more senses in addition to the five senses that are important for sensory integration and motor responses? These two senses are vestibular and proprioception:

Vestibular: the sensory system that helps us stay balanced, know which way we're facing, and feel how we move in relation to gravity. When our head moves, the tiny hairs in the inner ear detect the movement. That information is sent to the brain via the vestibular nerve. This helps us perceive that our head is changing directions and helps us keep our balance, such as when riding a bike.

Proprioception: the ability to perceive where our body is in space and how we're moving our different parts. Muscles, tendons, joints, and skin receive signals from the movement and pressure and send messages to the brain. This makes it possible to walk in a dark room without stumbling or enables us to complete an obstacle course without bumping into things.

All seven of our senses are constantly receiving information to help us navigate our environment. This information goes to the brain, which sorts it out and makes sense of it. We are not consciously thinking about sensory integration, but it's always happening. As it receives stimuli, the brain asks:

- What makes sense?
- What's important?
- What do I need to do?

The brain decides for you what's worth responding to and what's not. For example, if your child doesn't notice someone walking across the street, it's because their brain decided that piece of information is not important. This is called inattentional blindness.

Motor Integration

Motor integration is when the brain takes the sensory input that it has integrated and combines it with a motor response. This means the brain uses the information from the world around us to make our bodies move. Think about standing on a rocking ship. Your brain is synthesizing all the information it's receiving to keep you balanced on the deck, at least hopefully. This is why it can be easier to find your balance when you watch the horizon. You're giving your brain a solid piece of sensory information to focus on.

For your child with dyslexia, this is how they know what to do throughout their day. When they're sitting and reading in class, they can feel their feet on the floor to balance them and they can use their eyes to track the words that they're reading. If your child is having a hard time processing sensory information, they may be facing hurdles in addition to their dyslexia. This means that reading may be even more of a challenge.

What You Might Observe with Your Child

As you've learned, using multiple senses when learning something can be a valuable tool for your child to better understand lessons, such as the rules of language, so sensory and motor integration for your child is especially important. As children grow, we typically see their ability to integrate develop with them.

When we notice that a child's sensory and motor integration development isn't as expected, we should examine if challenges or delays are at play. Here are some examples of what sensory and motor integration challenges can look like:

- Complaining that certain fabrics are too itchy
- Not being interested in messy play
- Being afraid of going down a slide or climbing
- Consistently seeking out ways to move, like swings
- Being sensitive to loud noises
- Having difficulty listening in a noisy environment
- Avoiding or gagging on certain food textures or smells
- Difficulty holding a pencil
- Trouble zipping their jacket or tying their shoes
- Feeling overstimulated in social settings

If you've noticed your child displaying any of these behaviors or tendencies, it could be that sensory integration and motor integration are hurdles they need help overcoming. We'll look at four common challenge areas and strategies you can use at home to support your child's development. These four areas are:

- Sensory regulation
- Gross and fine motor skills
- Auditory processing
- Visual processing

CHALLENGE 1

Sensory Regulation

Sometimes emotion regulation (see chapter 6) and sensory regulation go hand in hand. That's because it can be much more difficult to regulate our emotions when our bodies are unregulated. When talking about sensory regulation in kids, there are three scenarios:

Sensory seeking: this is when our body is physically seeking something. This may mean that our brain cannot attend to whatever we're supposed to be doing.

Sensory avoidance: this is when we do something to lessen or stop experiencing whatever sense is too much for us. I often cover my ears when an ambulance goes by. Some people find fluorescent lighting painful to experience.

Sensory overload: this is when there is too much sensory information traveling to the brain and it reacts. This can look different for everyone, but it could be experiencing a meltdown, "bouncing off the walls," or simply shutting down and going silent and still.

In these scenarios, just like with emotion regulation, we can work to recognize what's happening in our bodies and employ strategies to help us regulate our senses and return our brains to a state where it can appropriately integrate the sensory information it's receiving. Unfortunately, for some kids, it's not so straightforward. If this is the case for your child with dyslexia, they can learn strategies to help.

Helps with

- Regulating sensory information going into the brain, helping your child feel calm and connected

What You'll Need

- Swings or spinning chair, if possible
- Weighted blanket
- Crunchy snacks, cold water
- Music and a speaker

When/Where

- Home
- Out and about with your child

If your child moves in ways that may not be appropriate for a situation they are in, their body may be seeking proprioceptive input to regulate their emotions and energy levels. These specific types of movements provide proprioceptive input:

- Big movements like jumping and pushing
- Deep pressure like hugs and weighted blankets
- Rhythmic movements like chewing and swinging

Of course, there are times during the day when it's not appropriate for your child to move like this or to receive deep pressure, especially in traditional school settings. If you notice your child moving in these ways more often than you might expect, they could be looking for ways to regulate their senses, and they can easily try these strategies in the proper settings.

Moving to Regulate

The movements in this approach can provide your child with the proprioceptive input they need to feel more regulated in their body. You can show these movements to your child, and they can determine what's most helpful. Be sure your child doesn't spend too much time on any one movement.

- Wall push-ups
- Hanging over the seat of a chair to apply pressure on the belly
- Inversion yoga poses like child's pose or downward dog to reset the nervous system
- Lying on the belly for grounding
- Swinging
- Spinning to activate the vestibular system (in the inner ear). Spinning to the right can be energizing or stimulating, while spinning to the left can be calming or grounding.

Changing the Sensory Input

If your child seems to be overwhelmed by the stimuli coming at them, look for ways to change the sensory input they are receiving to help their body reset and feel more regulated in the moment. Here are a few ideas:

- Chew on a crunchy snack.
- Drink cold water.
- Get a deep pressure hug.
- Watch a faraway moving object, like leaves in a tree.

Listening to Music

The vagus nerve is like a reset button for your nervous system. Music is a great way to activate that nerve because it's attached to the vocal cords. Here are a few ways you can use music to help your child regulate their senses:

- Sing, chant, or hum together.
- Listen to music. (Try different types and styles to see what resonates with your child.)
- Drum or tap with the beat.
- Dance together.

Tip: We just skimmed the potential challenge in sensory regulation. If these strategies aren't enough to help your child regulate, seek the guidance of a qualified occupational therapist.

CHALLENGE 2

Gross and Fine Motor Skills

Motor development is divided into two categories:

Gross motor skills are big movements that use big muscle groups. Examples include jumping, running, balancing, throwing, riding a bike, swimming, kicking a ball, and swinging. They are important because they:

- Build core strength and aid in posture.
- Help with coordination and balance.
- Create a foundation for fine motor movements.

Fine motor skills are small movements that use small muscle groups. Examples include using scissors, tying shoes, zipping a jacket, writing, using a fork, buttoning a shirt, and playing with blocks. They are important because they:

- Develop hand-eye coordination.
- Make it possible to care for oneself.
- Make writing possible and other academic tasks easier.

Both gross motor and fine motor skills play a huge role in your child's ability to successfully navigate their day. For example, children are often asked to sit on the carpet or at a desk to listen and work. If they're too focused on keeping their body upright because they do not have a strong core, they may not have the brainpower to attend to the teacher's lesson. The same can be true if they have difficulty writing and typing.

Helps with

- Building gross and fine motor skills

What You'll Need

- Pencil grips
- Weighted pencils
- Chunky writing tools
- Backrests for sitting on the floor

When/Where

- Home and free time

For a child to focus and concentrate on any task, it's essential for them to have the stability of a strong core. Here are a few signs to look out for that suggest your child's muscle tone or core strength needs improvement:

- Difficulty sitting on the floor
- Fidgeting
- Consistently slouching in a chair
- Preferring to sit in the W sitting position
- Seemingly clumsy
- Avoids physical activities like climbing, running, or kicking
- Struggles with handwriting
- Presses too hard or too lightly when writing
- Has a hard time dressing themselves
- Becomes easily frustrated with activities that require focus

If you have noticed any of these signs in your child, the following strategies can help. Encouraging core-building activities will go a long way in setting your child up for success, as building their gross motor skills can help them develop their fine motor skills.

Unstructured Play

Playing helps children figure out how to navigate the world. In particular, risky (but not dangerous) play challenges them to test their limits in age-appropriate ways. As they develop core strength and gross motor skills, their confidence in what their body can do increases.

Here are a few examples of risky, unstructured play in safe outdoor spaces with a few indoor options if safe outdoor spaces are unavailable:

- Climbing trees or jungle gyms
- Running, biking, or sledding
- Swinging high
- Digging, building, and playing in puddles and water
- Wrestling
- Rolling down hills
- Jumping jacks
- Crawling
- Bear or crab walks
- Frog jumps

Crossing the Body's Midline

Your child doesn't need to be enrolled in a long list of sports to build their gross motor skills. There are a few simple physical activities they can do at home. "Crossing the midline" is particularly effective. It involves moving a body part to the opposite side of the body.

Among its many benefits, crossing the midline builds connections between the two hemispheres of the brain and promotes core strength. There are fun activities you can find online that encourage crossing the body's midlines, but here are a few to get you started:

- Windmill arms
- Touching toes with your opposite hand
- Touching opposite knee with your elbow
- Crawling
- Dancing

Supportive Tools for Writing and Sitting

If your child is struggling with their fine motor skills, they may benefit from using a supportive writing tool. If your child's gross motor skills are a challenge and they have difficulty sitting on the floor when required, they may benefit from a backrest. Of course, sitting in a chair may help as well. There's no need to rush out and purchase all these items. Try one at a time to see if it helps. You can also talk with your child's teacher to see what might be available in the classroom to try at home. Here are a few examples of supportive tools to try:

- Pencil grips
- Chunky writing instruments
- Weighted pencils
- Folding backrest

Tip: You don't have to set aside a large chunk of time for daily exercise. Instead, focus on finding small moments in your day to be active with your child.

Eating and Mealtimes

There are biological differences between what it's like to eat as a kid and what it's like to eat as an adult. What you may think is delicious may be too spicy or taste "weird" to your child. Moreover, children's eating habits change over time. Whatever the case, it is normal for a child to sometimes be a "picky" eater. However, if your child is truly a reluctant eater, this is a challenge to address.

It's important to figure out why your child is avoiding certain foods or is generally having trouble around mealtimes. Here are some potential reasons:

- The texture or smell of the food turns them off.
- Their mouth may be sensitive because they're losing baby teeth.
- The physical act of chewing and swallowing is hard.
- They're not feeling regulated enough in their bodies to sit and eat.
- They're preoccupied with other thoughts.

If you ask your child why they don't want a particular food, they may be able to tell you; for example, "The chicken nuggets are scratchy and hurt my mouth." You can also look for patterns. Are there certain types of food they regularly find off-putting? Does it shift depending on the time of day or how they're feeling?

If your child is really struggling with chewing and swallowing, you may want to consult with a speech language pathologist who has special training in these areas. They can help your child develop the oral motor skills to chew and swallow their food.

CHALLENGE 3

Auditory Processing

Auditory processing is how our brains make sense of the sounds and speech we hear. For instance, a noise like a car horn tells us to get out of the way or that our ride is here. Processing speech enables us to respond to someone's questions, follow verbal instructions, and have conversations.

A person who continually struggles in this area may have an auditory processing disorder. Their hearing may be fine, but their brain struggles to interpret what they hear. While dyslexia is not an auditory processing disorder, it's not uncommon for children with dyslexia to also have this disorder. In fact, studies show that as much as 50 to 70 percent of people with dyslexia may also have an auditory processing disorder. Given that both disorders are, at their core, difficulties processing sounds and language, this makes sense.

To determine if this is a hurdle your child is facing, consider if your child exhibits any of these auditory processing challenges:

- Easily distracted or inattentive, especially in noisy environments
- Poor listening skills
- Difficulty learning new words or sounding out words when reading
- Difficulty following oral instructions

Helps with

- Following oral instructions, listening to someone talking

What You'll Need

- Something that makes noise remotely such as a phone or cricket noisemaker
- Noise-canceling headphones, white-noise machines, or nature sound playlist

When/Where

- Home

Auditory processing difficulties have two main impacts in the classroom: struggling to follow oral instructions and difficulty learning to read.

A person with auditory processing challenges hears everything at once because their brains struggle to identify, filter, organize, and attend to what they are hearing. In essence, the whirring of the air-conditioning system is just as important to their brain as the teacher talking. This makes it quite difficult for them to follow instructions, and they may become easily distracted by any noise they hear. The whole process can be exhausting for them. This can also have a knock-on effect with their reading. The brain may already be having a hard time distinguishing between different sounds, such as a doorbell versus a car horn. When we then ask an early reader to isolate the difference between "pat" and "bat," this may be almost impossible.

If you have noticed your child struggling with understanding what they hear, it may be because they need to build their auditory processing skills. Here are a few strategies that can help your child strengthen their listening skills.

Processing Sounds

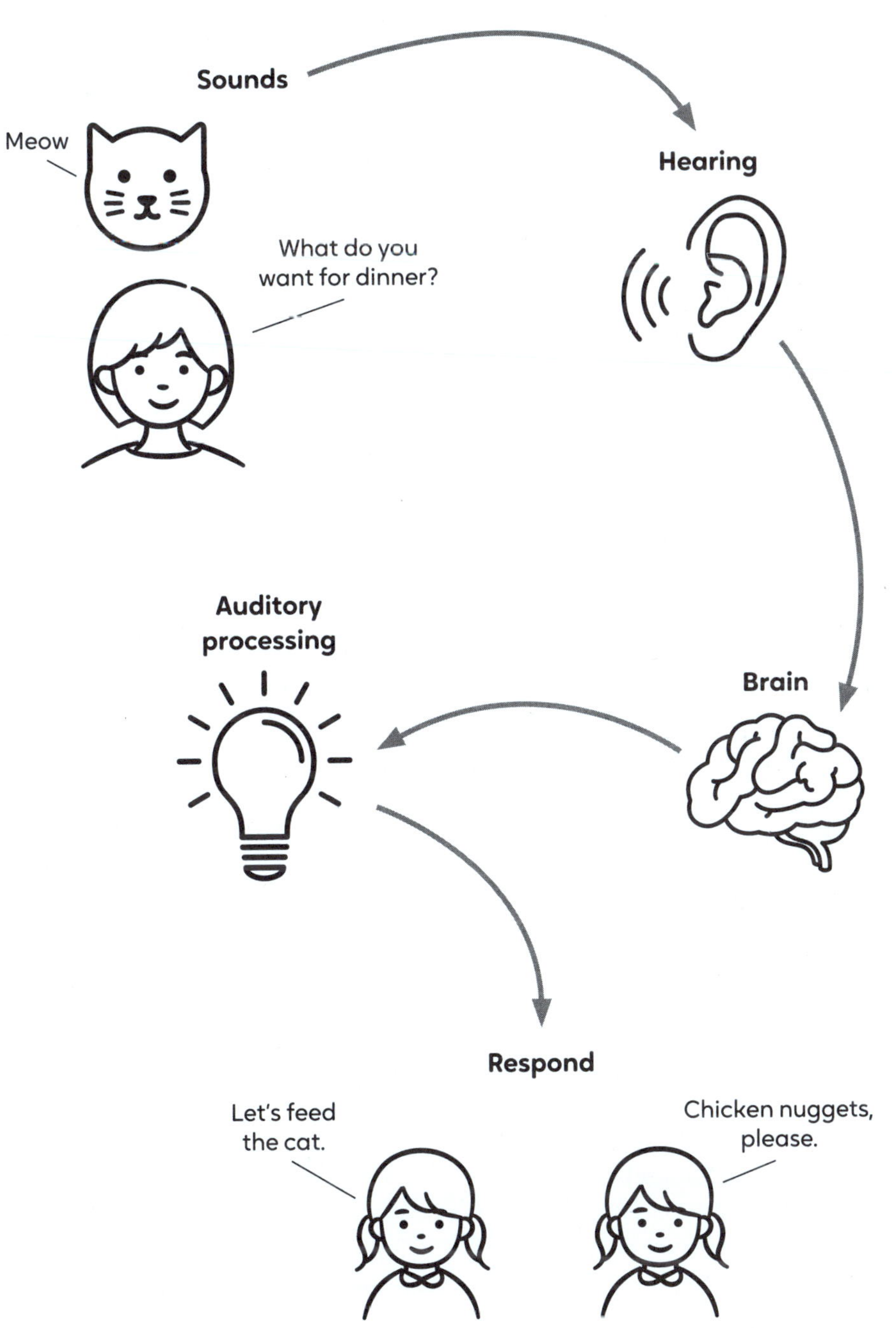

Practice Identifying and Locating Sounds

There are a variety of apps and online games to make listening practice fun, but here are two games to help your child practice identifying and locating sounds:

Guess my sound: Use your phone, your own voice, or items around the house to make different sounds. Ask your child to guess what noise they hear.

Hide-and-seek with sound: Ask your child to close their eyes while you place a noisemaking device that can be controlled remotely somewhere in the house. Count from 10 to zero and then turn on the noise. See if they can locate the noise. If this isn't challenging enough, you can pause and play music on a hidden Bluetooth speaker or on your phone.

First-Then Strategy

Whenever you need to give your child instructions but know they might struggle to process what you're asking, use a consistent sentence structure so that they know what to expect and in what order they need to accomplish what you're asking.

A great way to do this is to use the words "first" and "then" to give your child two instructions that go together. This can sound like:

- "First feed your pet fish, then wash your hands."
- "First read for 10 minutes, then have your snack."

Provide a Quiet Space

When asking your child to do something or when providing any important information, try to find a quiet space where they can better listen to you. The same goes for when they are doing homework or practicing their reading.

Rooms with carpets, pillows, and soft furniture absorb sound, so they make great conversation and study spaces. On the topic of studying, some children find noise-canceling headphones or white-noise machines helpful. You can usually also play white noise on smartphones.

While it may be difficult in a busy home, when speaking to your child, make an effort to:

- Minimize background noise.
- Shut the door to the room you are in.
- Keep other conversations to a minimum.

Tip: According to the Mayo Clinic, repeated ear infections is a risk factor for auditory processing disorder. If this is a concern of yours for your child, consult an ENT (ear/nose/throat) specialist or audiologist.

CHALLENGE 4

Visual Processing

Dyslexia is not a vision problem, and those with dyslexia don't see letters or words backward. Earlier, I also debunked the myth that colored overlays or special glasses help with dyslexia. While some people with dyslexia find reading certain fonts easier than others, research suggests that "dyslexia fonts" don't improve reading speed or comprehension. It could simply be a preference, or it could be because they have visual processing challenges in addition to their dyslexia. Like with an auditory processing challenge, a visual processing challenge is when the brain has a hard time making sense of the information it is receiving. The individual can see everything, but the brain struggles to understand what is being seen and how to respond.

It's important to think about whether visual processing is making reading even harder for your child with dyslexia. If you notice any of the challenges discussed later in this section when your child is doing an activity besides reading, they may have a visual processing challenge. In general, visual processing is the brain's ability to make sense of what the eyes are seeing and respond. This illustration depicts the role vision and visual processing play in catching a ball.

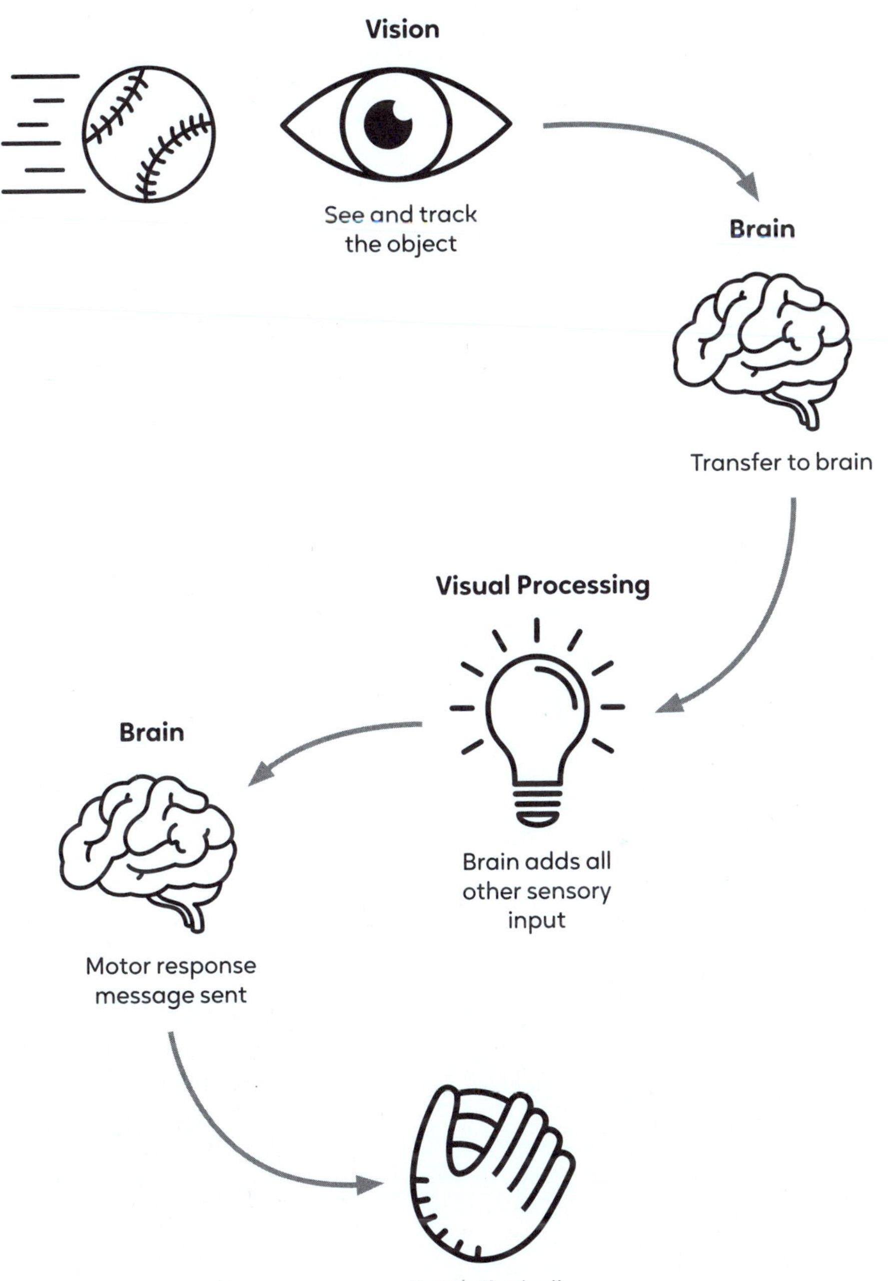
An Example of Vision and Visual Processing
Vision
See and track the object
Brain
Transfer to brain
Visual Processing
Brain adds all other sensory input
Brain
Motor response message sent
Catch the ball

If your child is having a hard time processing what they are seeing, reading words on a page is going to be even more difficult. Here are some reading and writing challenges that may stem from visual processing delays:

- Tracking while reading—skipping lines and skipping words
- Seeing letters "swimming" on the page
- Difficulty understanding what is written on the board
- Having a hard time reading when there's a lot of decoration on a page
- Not knowing where to start writing on a page
- Writing parts of sentences on different lines

Helps with

- Reading accurately, orienting words on a page, and hand-eye coordination

What You'll Need

- Slant board
- Index cards or rulers
- Blue paper
- Tweezer or chopsticks
- Balls

When/Where

- Reading and writing tasks at home
- Sports and activities

A child with visual processing disorder *without* a diagnosis of dyslexia is usually on track with their speech development and phonological awareness. They usually know their letter/sound correspondences at the same developmental milestones as their peers. Despite this, their reading is not accurate, especially when there is more text to read. A few things can help improve accuracy:

- Reading a book or page at an angle
- Reading a book or page closer to one's face
- Using a card to track lines

It's important to determine if there are other factors impacting your child's reading development. If you've noticed your child do any of the following, they may also be experiencing visual processing difficulties:

- Wanting to move the book or page closer to their face
- Holding the book or page at different angles
- Squinting
- Tilting their head when reading or writing

There are several strategies that can help improve the visual processing challenges a child with dyslexia might also be facing.

"Quick Fixes" for Paper-Based Activities

Children with visual processing challenges may benefit from any or all of the following suggestions. Be patient and flexible as you help your child discover what works best for them.

- Reading with the page or book at different angles and/or distances

- Using a larger font for printouts
- Printing on light blue paper
- Writing on a slant board (or sloped surface)

You don't have to purchase a slant board to get the benefit of a sloped surface. You can use a three-ring binder, a sticky pad, and a clipboard. Experiment with different binder widths to see what slope works best for your child. Once you find the right size, ask your child's teacher if they can also use a sloped surface at school.

Develop and Improve Hand-Eye Coordination

To help your child develop their visual processing abilities, you can find fun ways for your child to work on their hand-eye coordination. Ask your child for their ideas of what they might find fun, but here are a few to get them started:

- Throwing and catching a ball
- Stringing beads
- Origami (folding objects out of paper)
- Riding a bike or scooter
- Jumping rope
- Using chopsticks or tweezers to pick up small objects
- Team sports like softball, volleyball, or soccer

Tracking while Reading and Limiting Visual Input

Tracking is the ability to follow lines of text across a page, smoothly and accurately, without losing our place as we read.

This helps us read the words and lines in the right order. If your child with dyslexia is also skipping words or lines, it becomes that much more difficult to understand what they are reading. If this is a struggle for your child, here are some ways to help them better track:

- Use their finger to track each word as they read. (Accessories such as fake fingers can make tracking more fun. Refer to the QR code on page 233 for more visual references.)
- Move a large plain index card down the page to track which line to read.
- Create blank space by using blank paper or index cards to cover up the parts of the page or worksheet that aren't being focused on at that time.
- Use reading guide highlighter strips to focus on specific words or lines of text.

Tip: An occupational or therapeutic optometrist can conduct a thorough eye examination to see if visual processing challenges are impacting your child's development and if they are a candidate for vision therapy.

System Overload: Tantrum or Meltdown?

It's normal for kids to have big reactions to something, but navigating those reactions can be tricky for a parent or caregiver. However, when you understand what your child is trying to communicate with their behavior and that they may have no control over how they are acting, you are in a better place to help them regulate.

Tantrums and meltdowns are different types of emotional reactions, although a tantrum can turn into a meltdown. Knowing how to identify each one better equips you to help your child. The table below illustrates the differences and how best to respond.

	Tantrum	Meltdown
What it is	Tantrums are an outburst that is a method of communication and often a choice to act that way while the child is still in control of their actions.	A meltdown is an uncontrolled reaction in which the prefrontal cortex "shuts down" and the child is not in control of their actions.
What it looks like	During a tantrum, the child may look for reactions from others; yelling, screaming, stomping, whining, and/or throwing objects.	A meltdown is usually preceded by signs of distress: yelling, lashing out, running away, or shutting down.
What causes it	Tantrums are typically frustration-based and caused by being denied something they want.	Meltdowns are fight-or-flight reactions to sensory overwhelm, a specific event, fatigue, fear, or a feeling.
What stops it	Tantrums typically stop when the child receives what they want or calms down.	Meltdowns stop when the sensory input has changed, the child has worn themselves out, or the fear has passed.

Reflection

After implementing a variety of sensory and motor integration strategies with your child, hit pause and reflect on how far you've come in this journey. Even if it isn't immediately clear, just engaging in these exercises means that you and your child are making progress. Here are some questions to guide your reflection:

What wins, great or small, have you noticed?

____

____

____

____

What daily task is your child now able to do independently?

____

____

____

____

How much more confident is your child in their own abilities?

____

____

____

____

What moments of joy have these strategies brought you and your child?

What do you better understand about your child now regarding their struggles or behaviors?

How are you better able to support your child now?

What have you done to step back and keep yourself regulated during moments of frustration?

____

____

____

____

____

Which of these strategies do you think your child's teacher would find helpful and why?

____

____

____

____

____

Conclusion

As you reach the end of this book, take pride in the amazing work you've put in to support your child's learning journey. You've learned what dyslexia and any coexisting conditions can mean for your child and how to support them at home with fun and helpful strategies. You are priming your child to learn, grow, and flourish!

As I've stressed throughout this book, every child and every family is unique. What has specifically worked for you, your child, and your family? Which discussions most resonated with you? Which strategies did you find most effective? Which of the strategies were among your child's favorites? How can you continue to build on these areas to stay on track as your child ages and continues on their academic path?

It's important to remember that dyslexia is a lifelong journey. What your child needs to grow and be successful will shift over time. Each phase of their academic career will look different as the demands grow. You may need to revisit some of the strategies or use the resources at the end of this book to support your child as they move toward their teenage years and beyond. Your child's school and their support team will always be resources for you as well.

Finally, I want you to remember to focus on your own power and strength. There will be bumps in the road, but you are now armed with knowledge and empowered with strategies. You know your child, and there are resources and professionals to help. You got this!

References

Books

Brown, B. (2017). *Rising Strong: How the Ability to Reset Transforms the Way We Live, Love, Parent, and Lead.* Random House.

Bruner, J. S. (1966). *Toward a Theory of Instruction*. Harvard University Press.

Chabris, C. F., & Simons, D. (2010). *The Invisible Gorilla: How Our Intuitions Deceive Us*. Crown.

Dweck, C. S. (2006). *Mindset: The New Psychology of Success.* Random House.

Eide, B. L., & Eide, F. F. (2011). *The Dyslexic Advantage: Unlocking the Hidden Potential of the Dyslexic Brain.* Hudson Street Press.

Haidt, J. (2024). *The Anxious Generation: How the Great Rewiring of Childhood Is Causing an Epidemic of Mental Illness.* Penguin Press.

Shaywitz, S. E., & Shaywitz, J. R. (2020). *Overcoming Dyslexia: Second Edition, Completely Revised and Updated* (Illustrated ed.). Alfred A. Knopf.

Wexler, N. (2019). *The Knowledge Gap: The Hidden Cause of America's Broken Education System—and How to Fix It.* Avery.

Wolf, M. (2008). *Proust and the Squid: The Story and Science of the Reading Brain.* HarperCollins.

Journal Articles

Gough, P. B., & Tunmer, W. E. (1986). "Decoding, Reading, and Reading Disability." *Remedial and Special Education, 7*(1), 6–10. doi.org/10.1177/074193258600700104.

Hoover, W. A., & Gough, P. B. (1990). "The Simple View of Reading." *Reading and Writing: An Interdisciplinary Journal, 2*(2), 127–160. doi.org/10.1007/BF00401799.

Odegard, T. N., & Dye, M. (2024). "The Gift of Dyslexia: What Is the Harm in It?" *Annals of Dyslexia, 74,* 143–157. doi.org/10.1007/s11881-024-00308-9.

Scarborough, H. S. (2001). "Connecting Early Language and Literacy to Later Reading (Dis)Abilities: Evidence, Theory, and Practice." In S. B. Neuman & D. K. Dickinson (Eds.), *Handbook of Early Literacy Research*. The Guilford Press.

Government Reports

National Institute of Child Health and Human Development (2000). *Report of the National Reading Panel: Teaching Children to Read: An Evidence-Based Assessment of the Scientific Research Literature on Reading and Its Implications for Reading Instruction.* U.S. Government Printing Office. nichd.nih.gov/sites/default/files/publications/pubs/nrp/documents/report.pdf.

Office of Special Education and Rehabilitative Services, U.S. Department of Education (July 2000). *A Guide to the Individualized Education Program*. ed.gov/sites/ed/files/parents/needs/speced/iepguide/iepguide.pdf.

Podcast

Hanford, E. (Host). (2022). *Sold a Story: How Teaching Kids to Read Went So Wrong* [Audio podcast]. APM Reports. features.apmreports.org/sold-a-story.

Resources

Websites

Cognitive Connections

efpractice.com

This practice of certified speech-language pathologists, occupational therapists, and special educators offers a range of supports and products to help learners develop executive functioning skills.

High Noon Books

highnoonbooks.academictherapy.com

This niche publishing company offers decodable readers and high-interest, low-level books for those whose reading level is not the same as their maturity level. You can find a wide range of interesting books at your child's level to get them hooked on reading.

The International Dyslexia Association (IDA)

dyslexiaida.org

This great resource offers research-based information, evidence-based approaches, community, and advocacy for those with dyslexia and their families. They also keep a database of dyslexia support professionals.

LD Online

ldonline.org

LD Online is an informative website about learning disabilities and differences where you can find helpful information on dyslexia and a range of other disorders.

Reading Rockets: Launching Young Readers

readingrockets.org

Reading Rockets is a great resource for parents and teachers, providing accurate tips, strategies, and expert advice about teaching all children to read, including struggling readers and those with dyslexia. This is also a great resource to learn more about phonological awareness.

State of Dyslexia

stateofdyslexia.org

From the National Center on Improving Literacy, this resource provides a state-by-state breakdown of enacted dyslexia-focused education laws, teacher certifications, and state-approved resources related to dyslexia support in the United States. This is a great reference to better understand your child's legal rights and what resources are approved in your state.

Understood

understood.org

Understood is the leading nonprofit provider of accurate information on dyslexia and other learning and thinking differences. Their free resources and articles are extensive and can answer almost all your questions.

University of Florida Literacy Institute

ufli.education.ufl.edu

Offers free resources aligned with the science of reading, including downloadable grapheme cards: ufli.education.ufl.edu/wp-content/uploads/2022/09/UFLI_Grapheme_Cards.pdf.

Wrightslaw Special Education Law and Advocacy

wrightslaw.com

This website offers resources on special education law.

The Yale Center for Dyslexia & Creativity (YCDC)

dyslexia.yale.edu

The YCDC is a top go-to resource for the latest research, expert advice, and reliable support to help people with dyslexia thrive.

Books

Dyslexia Is My Superpower (Most of the Time) by Margaret Rooke (Jessica Kingsley Publishers, 2017)

This fun book is a collection of real-life interviews from kids aged eight to eighteen on what it's like to have dyslexia. They share their personal tips and strategies for letting their creative side go wild and how doing so has helped them be successful in school.

The Dyslexic Advantage: Unlocking the Hidden Potential of the Dyslexic Brain by Brock L. Eide, MD, MA, and Fernette F. Eide, MD (Hudson Street Press, 2011)
This uplifting book about the possible advantages of having a dyslexic brain highlights the true-life stories of 18 impressive, successful adults with dyslexia.

Fish in a Tree by Lynda Mullaly Hunt (Nancy Paulsen Books, 2015)
The fictional story of Ally, a bright student who hides her reading troubles, explores the struggles and emotions of a child with dyslexia. Through the support of a caring teacher and new friendships, Ally begins a journey of self-discovery, self-confidence, and embracing her unique strengths.

Scan this QR code for further resources, downloadable templates, and more.

Index

T

V

W

Acknowledgments

Writing this book has been an incredible journey, and I am deeply grateful to the many people who have inspired, supported, and guided me along the way.

To start with, thank you to my family and friends for your unwavering support. Anna, for always being my sounding board. Daniel, for bravely sharing your own story as inspiration. Rosemary, for never hesitating to share your honest opinions. Your love and encouragement have meant everything to me.

To my professional mentors and colleagues, I am especially grateful to the team at Neuhaus Education Center for their dedication to training educators and dyslexia specialists. Your work has shaped and strengthened my understanding of how to best support students with dyslexia. To the researchers whose work has expanded our collective knowledge of dyslexia, literacy, cognitive functions, and child development, I deeply appreciate your contributions to this field.

To those who have inspired and shaped this book, I am endlessly grateful. Kate, for your honest and open feedback. Heather, for being an inspiration in the way you see and uplift children. Mallary, for your expertise and suggestions. Erica, for being one of the most heartening teachers I've crossed paths with. And to the countless educators I've had the privilege of working with, your passion and dedication continue to inspire me.

Finally, to every student, parent, and caregiver I've had the honor of supporting—your resilience, curiosity, and determination are the heart of this book. Thank you for allowing me to be part of your journey.

About the Author

Rebecca Bush is a dedicated dyslexia interventionist with nearly two decades of experience. Passionate about transforming literacy education, she empowers children with dyslexia and their families by blending evidence-based instruction with practical parenting strategies to create meaningful, lasting change.

She offers tailored parent coaching, individualized intervention programs, and school consultations, focusing on personalized support. She works closely with families and schools to ensure every child has the resources, confidence, and skills they need to succeed.

Rebecca holds an MEd in advanced literacy from Concordia University of Texas and an MA in elementary education from the University of Alabama. She earned her undergraduate degree at the University of California, Berkeley, and completed the Dyslexia Specialist Preparation Program at Neuhaus Education Center.

As a certified academic language therapist (Academic Language Therapy Association) and licensed dyslexia therapist (Texas Department of Licensing and Regulation), Rebecca is also a certified reading specialist and special needs teacher (Texas Education Agency). In addition, she is a professional/specialist member of the International Dyslexia Association. Rebecca enjoys spending time with animals and provides equine-assisted services.

For more information, visit leadchanges.com.

Hi there,

We hope *Dyslexia and Your Newly Diagnosed Child* helped you. If you have any questions or concerns about your book, or have received a damaged copy, please contact customerservice@penguinrandomhouse.com. We're here and happy to help.

Also, please consider writing a review on your favorite retailer's website to let others know what you thought of the book.

Sincerely,

The Zeitgeist Team